Family Cats

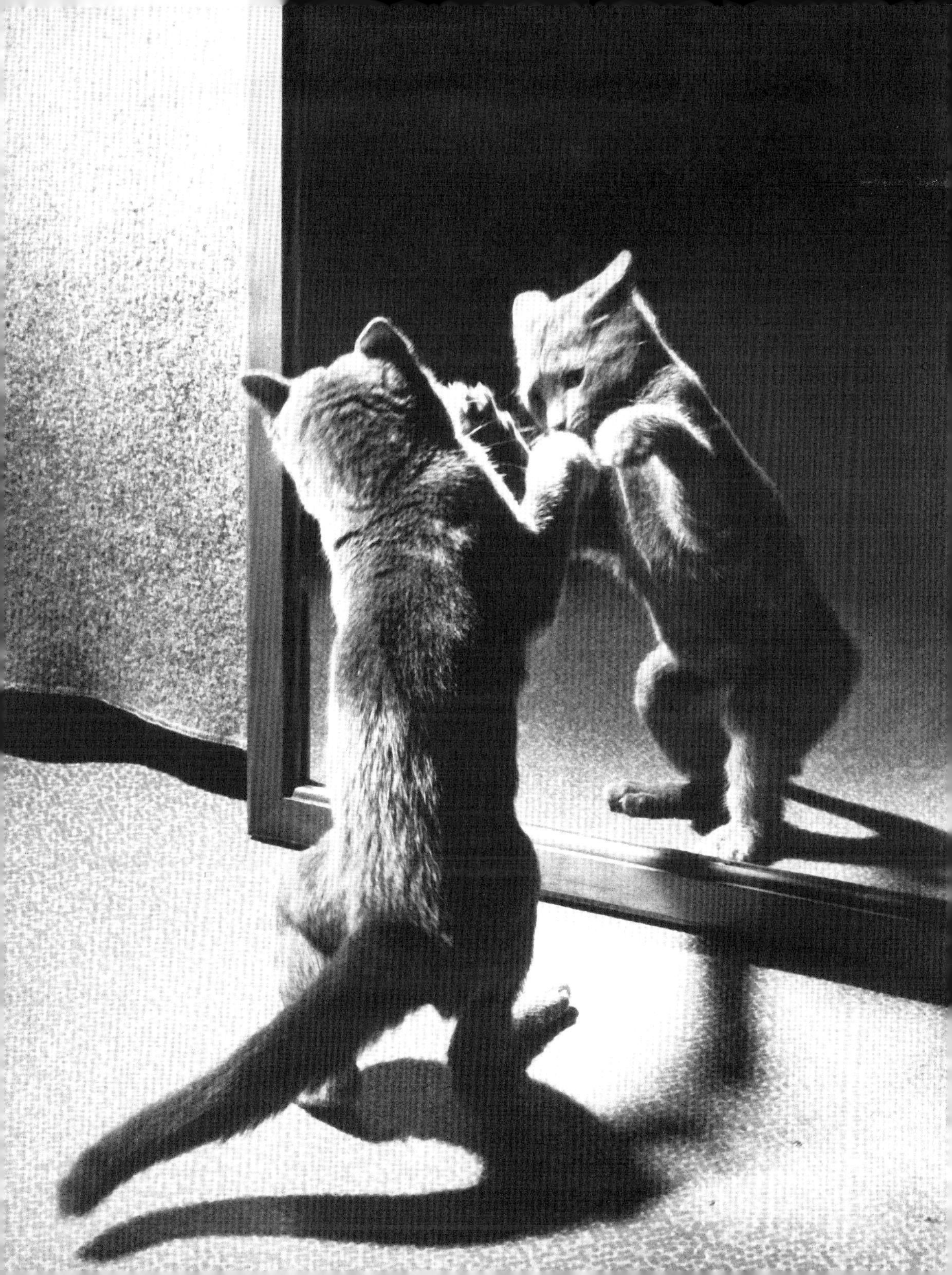

FOREWORD

Cats!

They drive you crazy and they blind you with love. I have been addicted since an early age, when I used to play with all the feral felines living behind my parents' seaside hotel in North Wales.

It's not that I am dissatisfied with my own cats - I have three extremely beautiful Persians that I love dearly. Blanket (from Michael Jackson's son,) Blondie (the singer), and Jimi (as in Hendrix). But looking at all the cute kittens in Walter Chandoha's book brings out the mother instinct in me. The joy of owning a kitten, watching it grow, and of course if you are Walter photographing it, is beyond words.

I think one of the reasons my first marriage fell apart was because I was not allowed a cat in the house as my husband was highly allergic. So when my second marriage fell apart (not because of the cats) the only thing that I demanded in the settlement was our two gorgeous British Blues, Brian and Stanley. Then I had two Tabbies Maureen and Daureen, right up until I relocated to America 40 years ago.

Since moving here I have lived happily with my partner and fellow cat lover Didier. We started our family with two Chartreux - Coco (Chanel) and Henri (Leconte), followed a bit later by Madame Grey (or Baby for short).

As the years passed we added to our family with Puff Puff, a great big fluffy ginger tomcat. Then came little Bart, who I found on the internet while casting cats for a *Vogue* fashion story. He was my first real Persian and the love of my life. I was hooked. I visited the cat show at Madison Square Garden and made a beeline for all the long haired breeds - Persians, Rag Dolls etc and found Pumpkin. Which brings us up to today with Blanket, Blondie and Jimi.

I wish I had met Walter, for not only do we have a shared love of cats, but my day job for the last 50 years has been working with photographers (although mostly fashion photographers). I have a large photography collection, including many pictures that feature cats (I even own one by Irving Penn, and several by Edward Weston). Walter and I would certainly have had a big connection.

What a wonderful life Walter must have had, surrounded by all his muses... his wife Maria, his children and his cats. I particularly love his humorous pictures. I smile every time I see his little clown kitten laughing at the camera. Or Loco boxing himself in front of the mirror, like a real pro. Seen through Walter's lens you feel each cat personality beaming out, an endless supply of leaping, bounding, yawning kittens at his disposal. I envy him!!

Grace Coddington

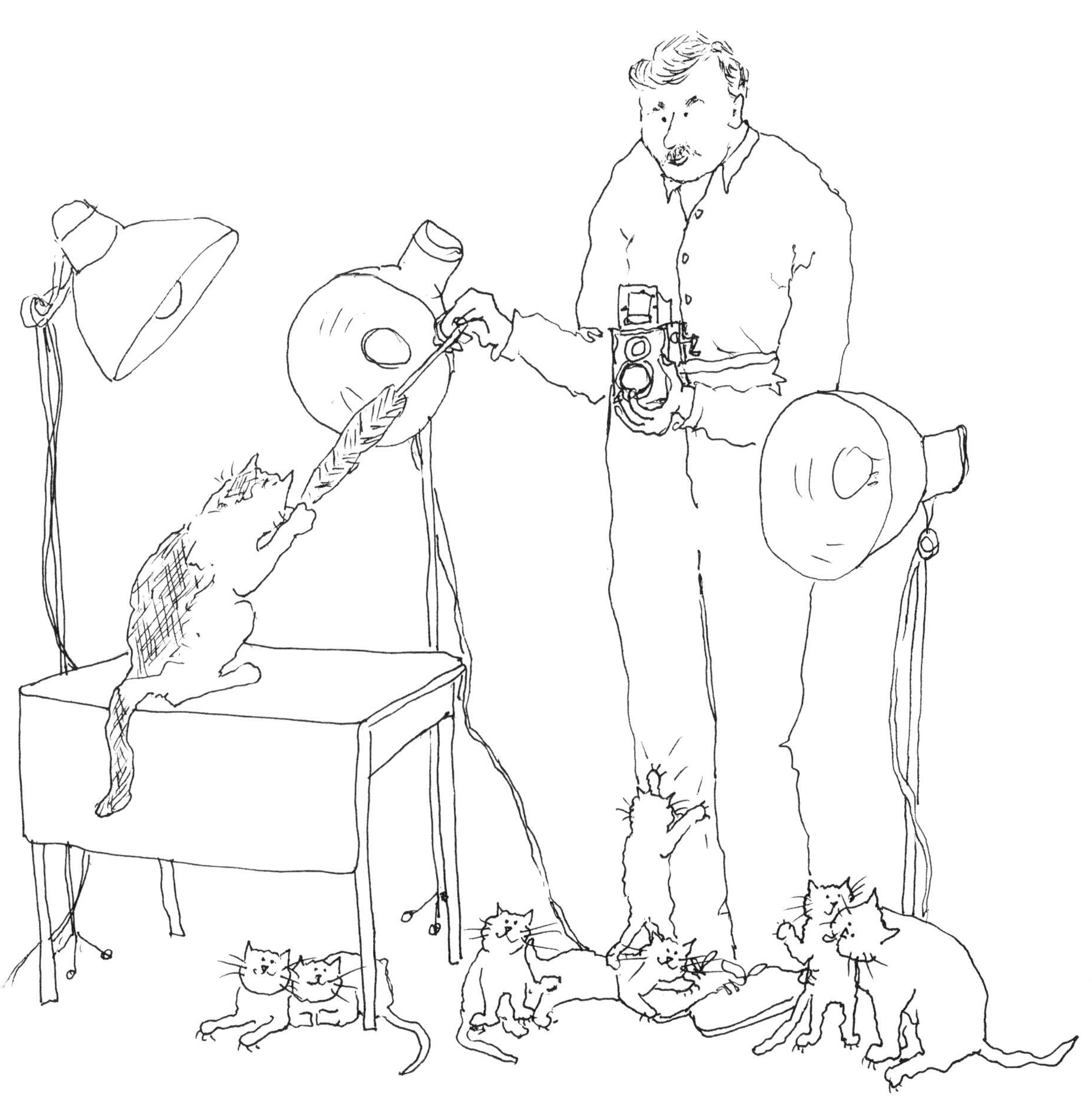

ILLUSTRATION BY GRACE CODDINGTON

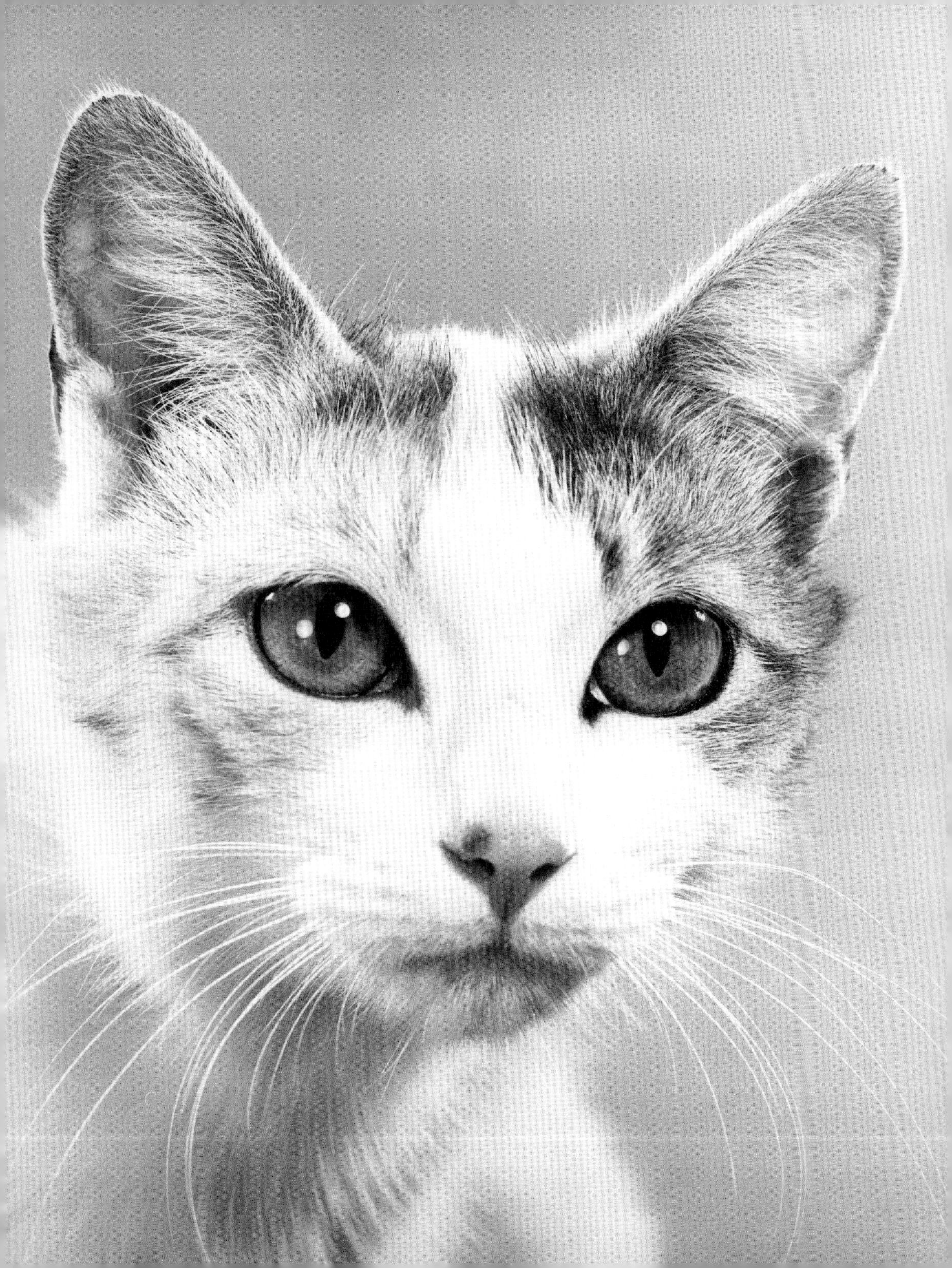

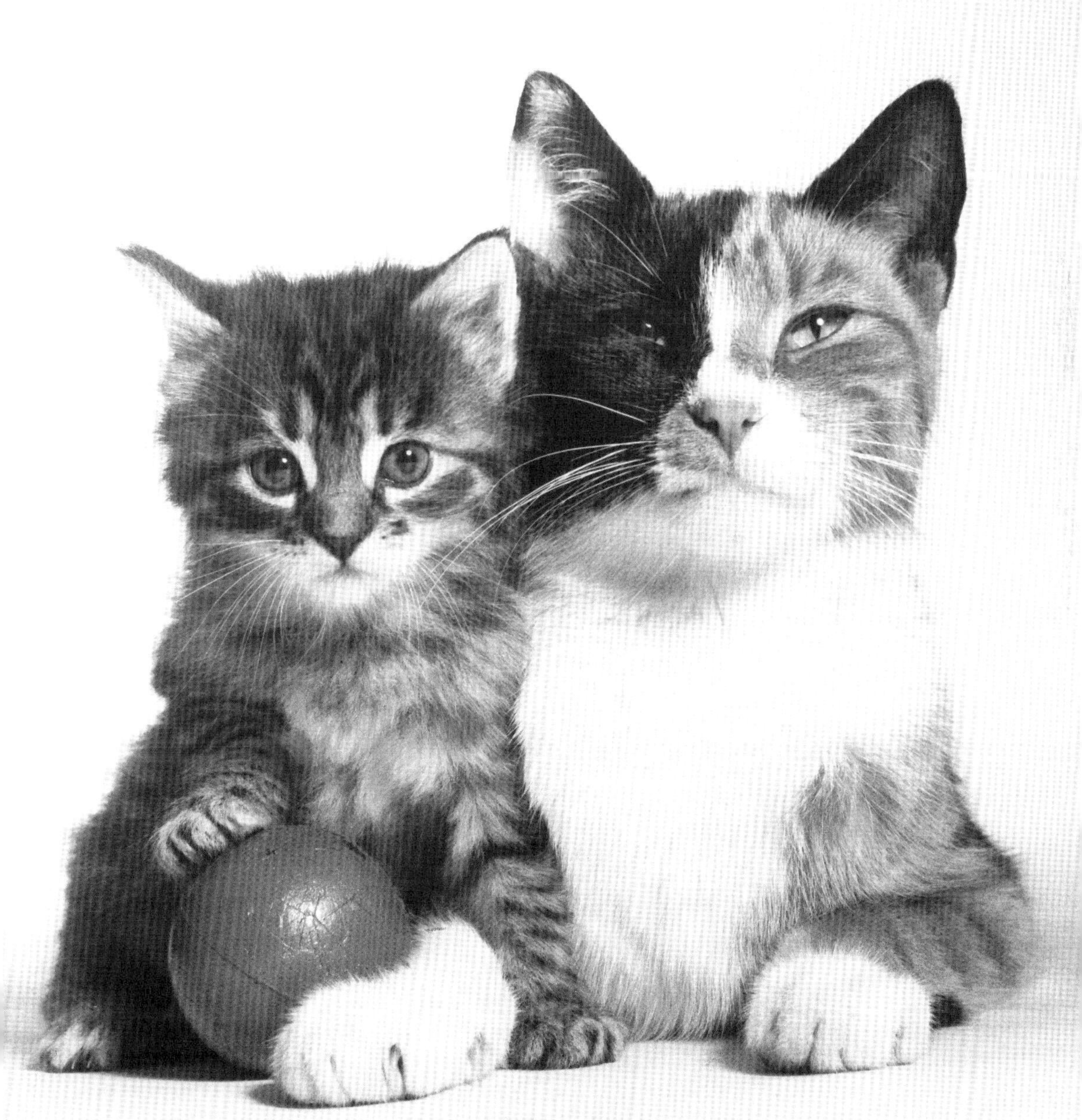

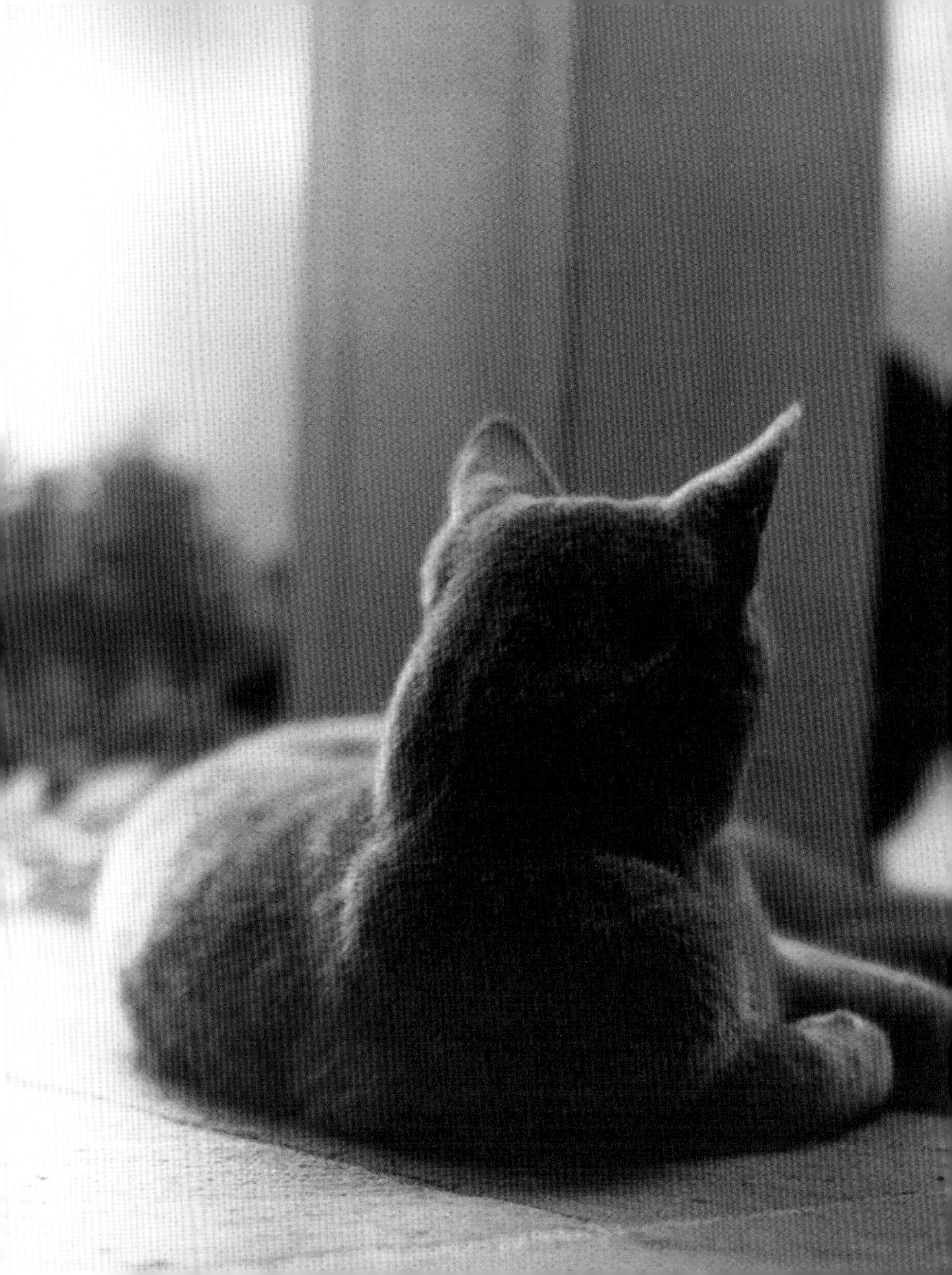

Previous pages
▲ LONG ISLAND, 1957
▲ LONG ISLAND, 1956

◄ LOCO, NEW JERSEY, 1961

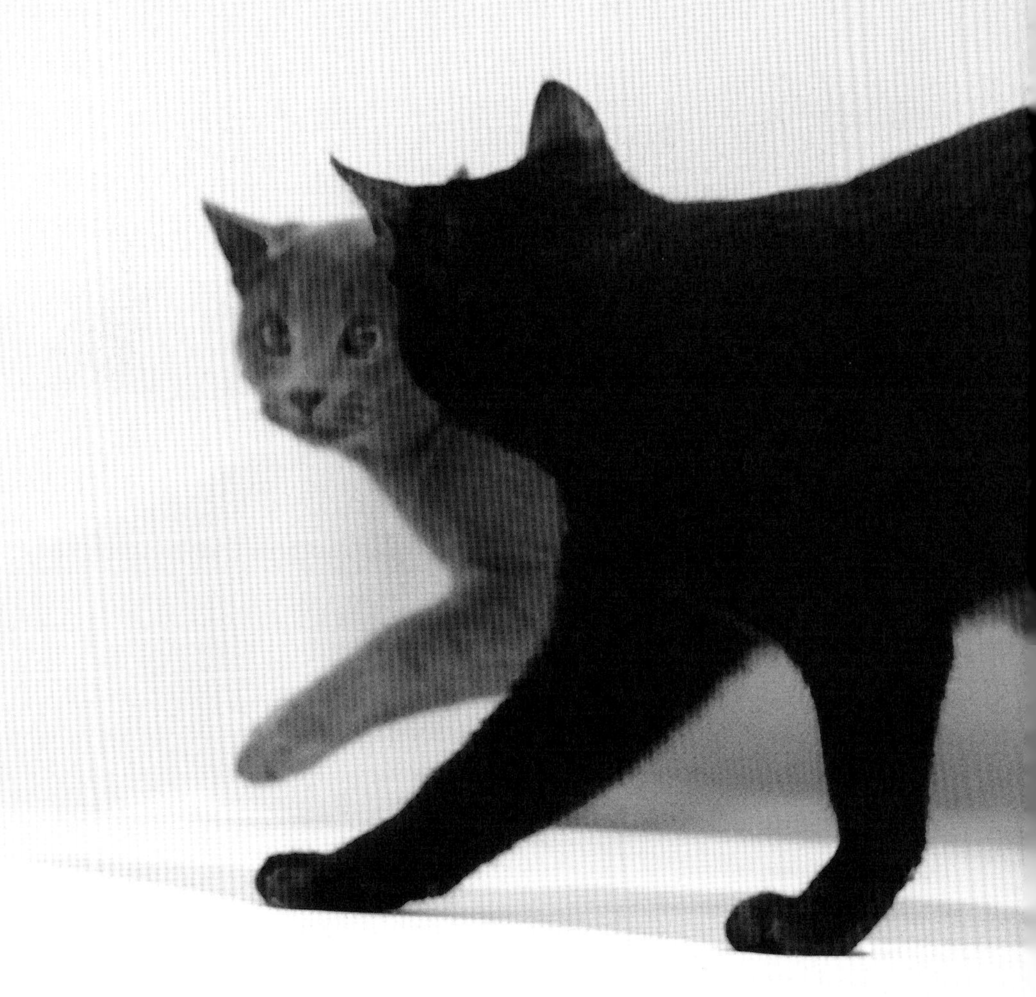

LOCO & JET, LONG ISLAND, 1952

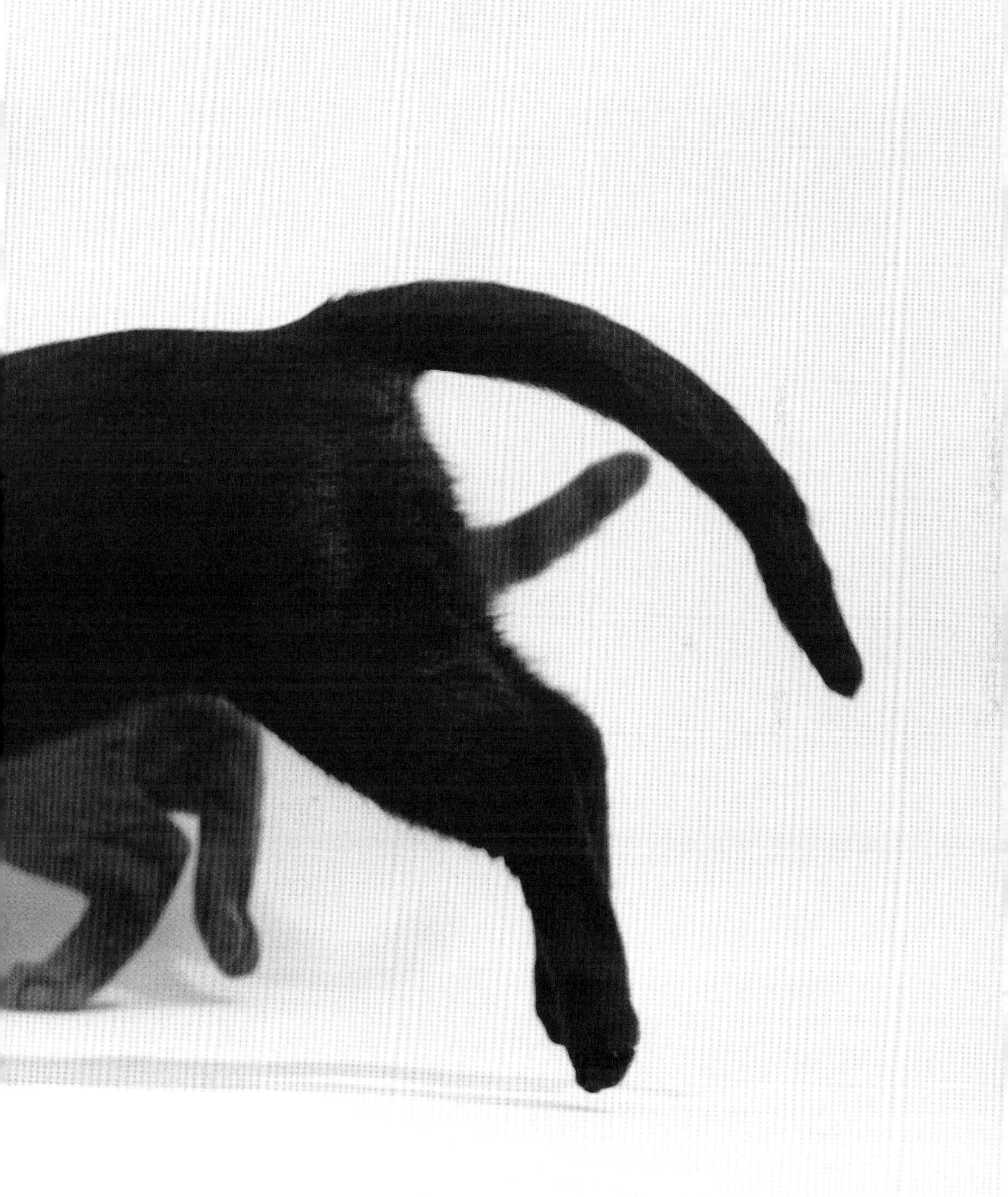

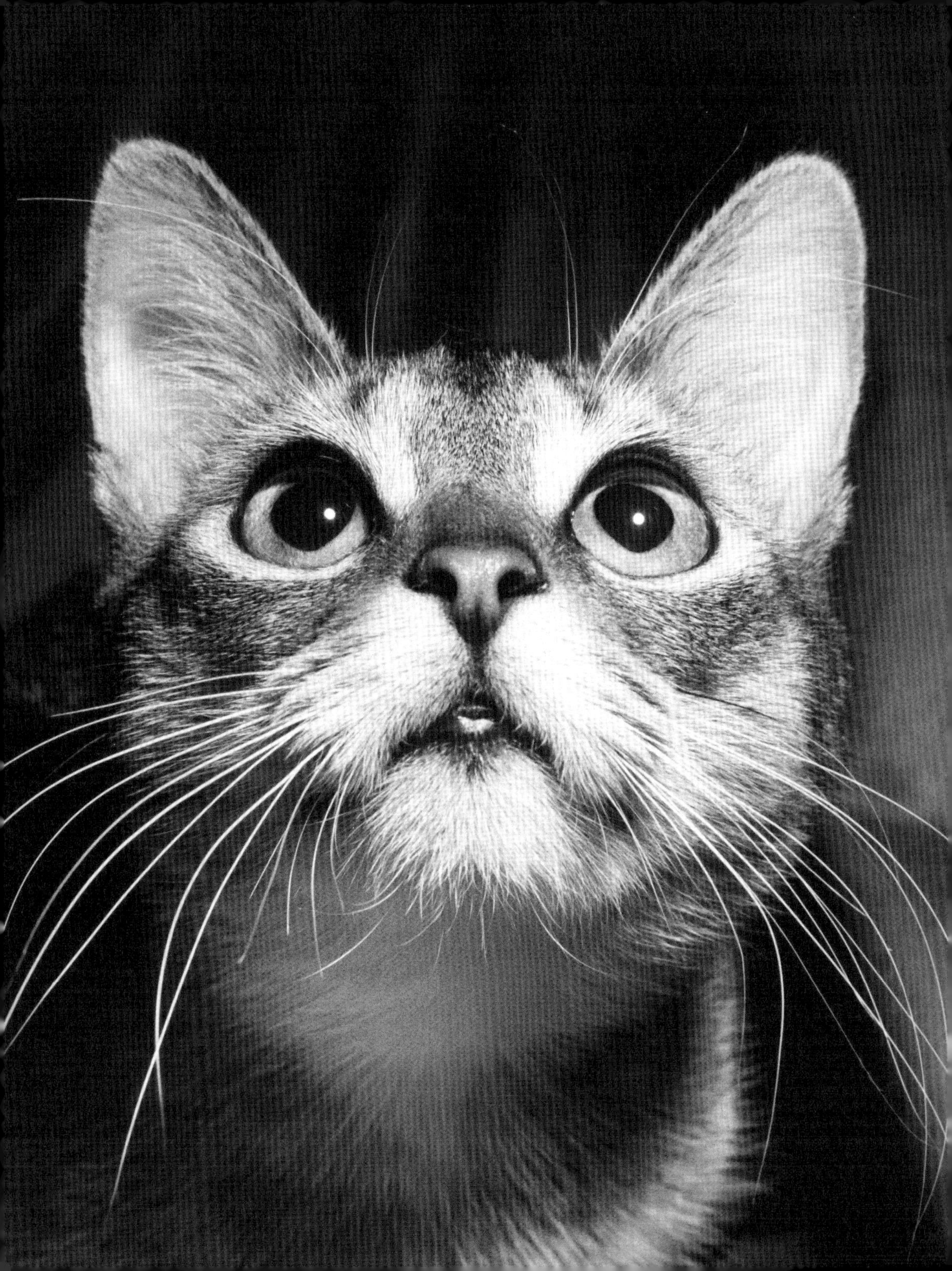

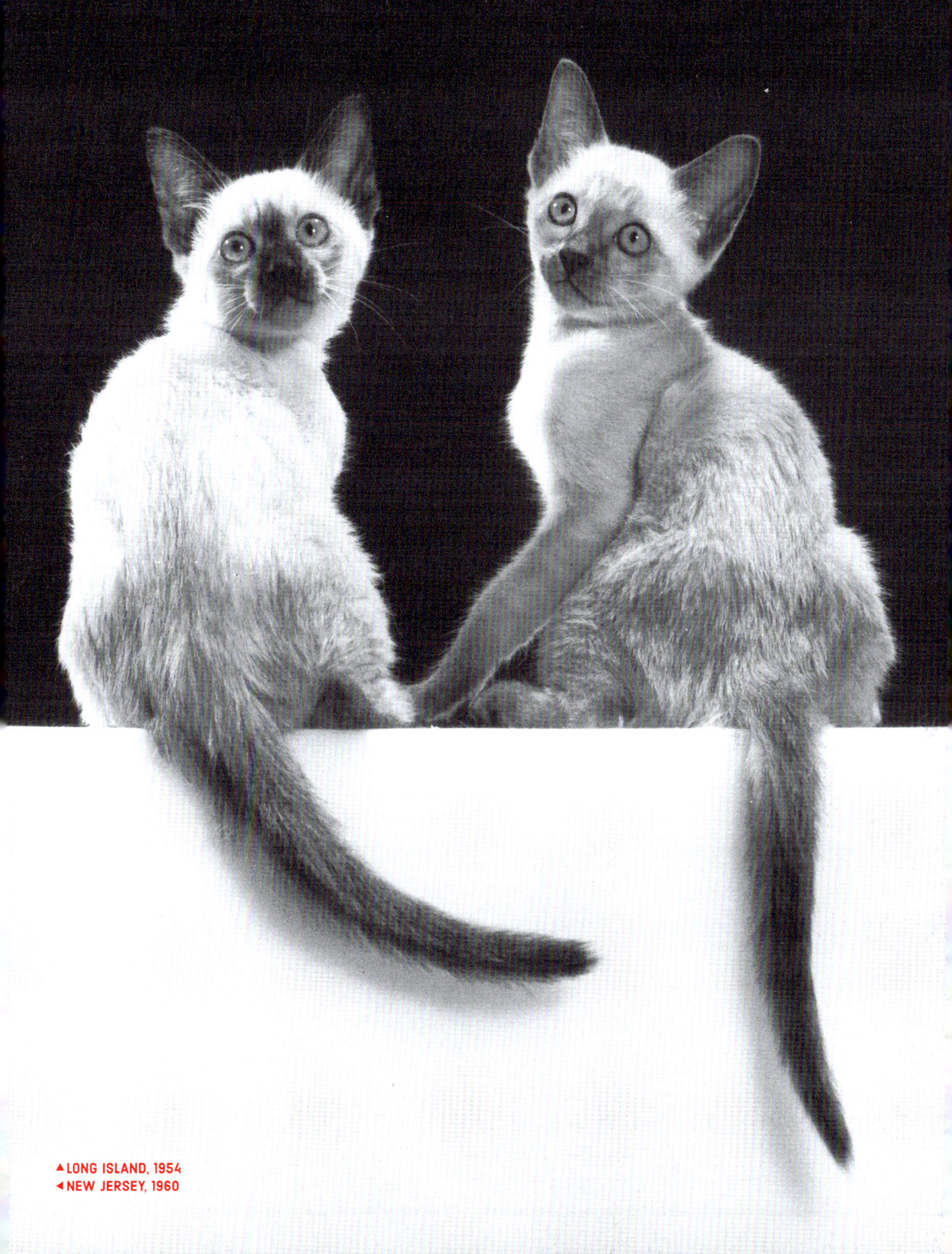

▲LONG ISLAND, 1954
◄NEW JERSEY, 1960

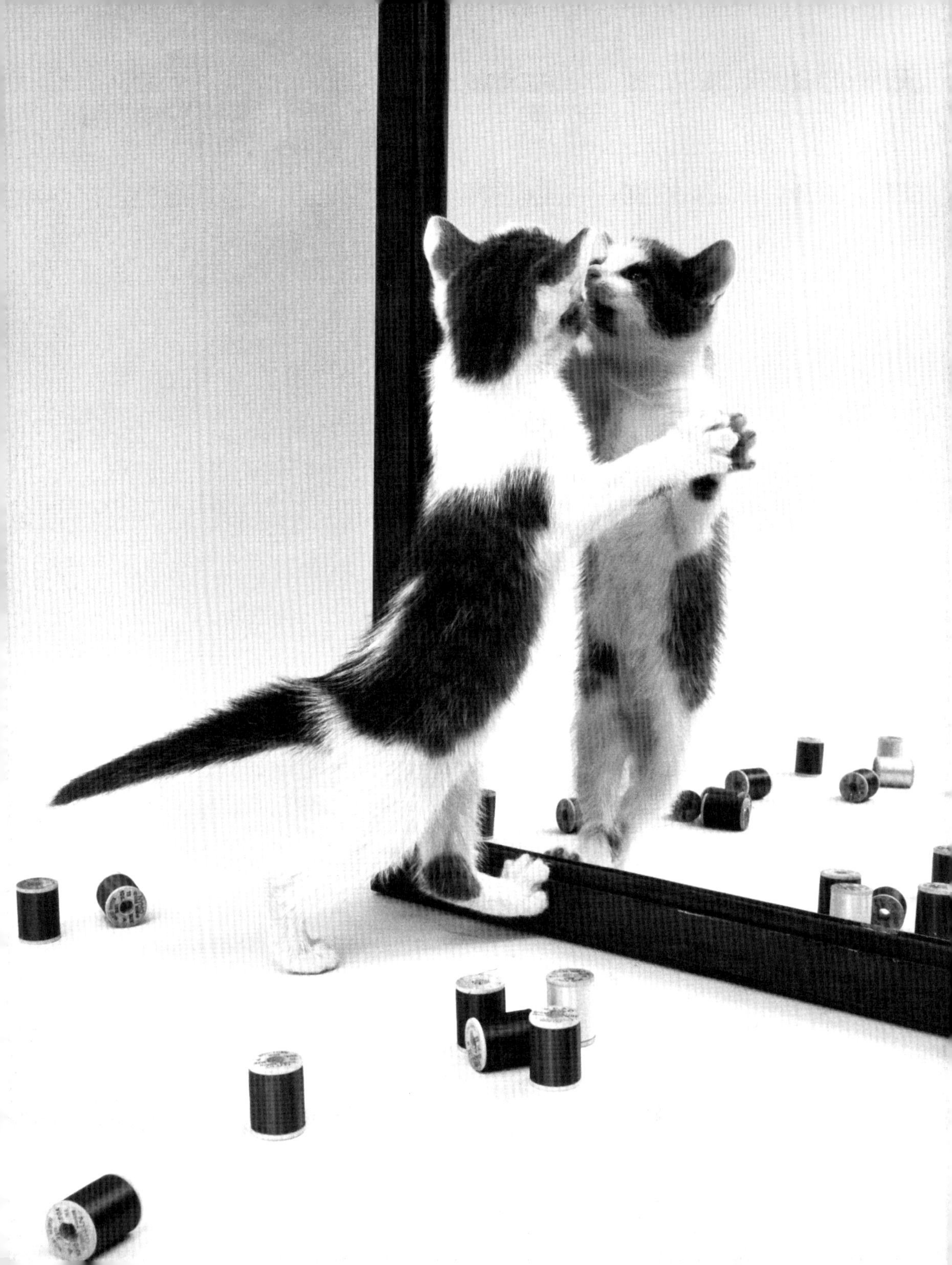

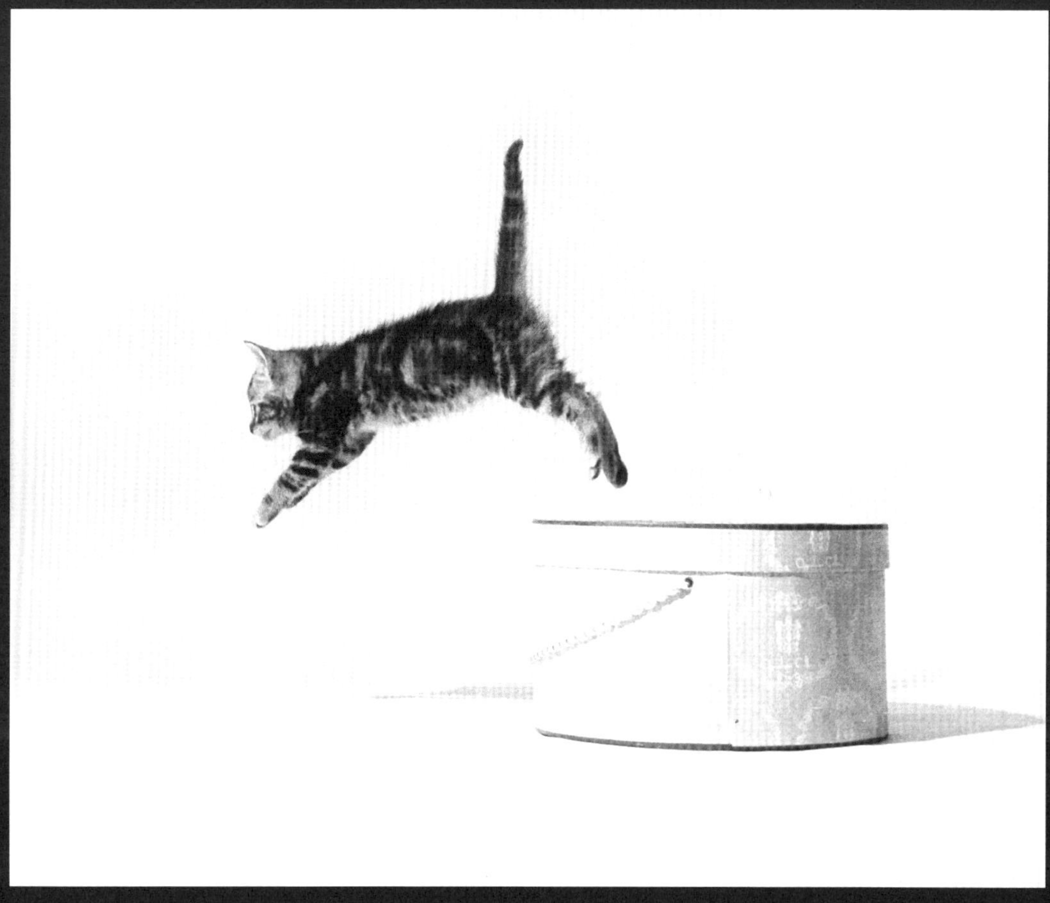

▲ NEW YORK CITY, 1951

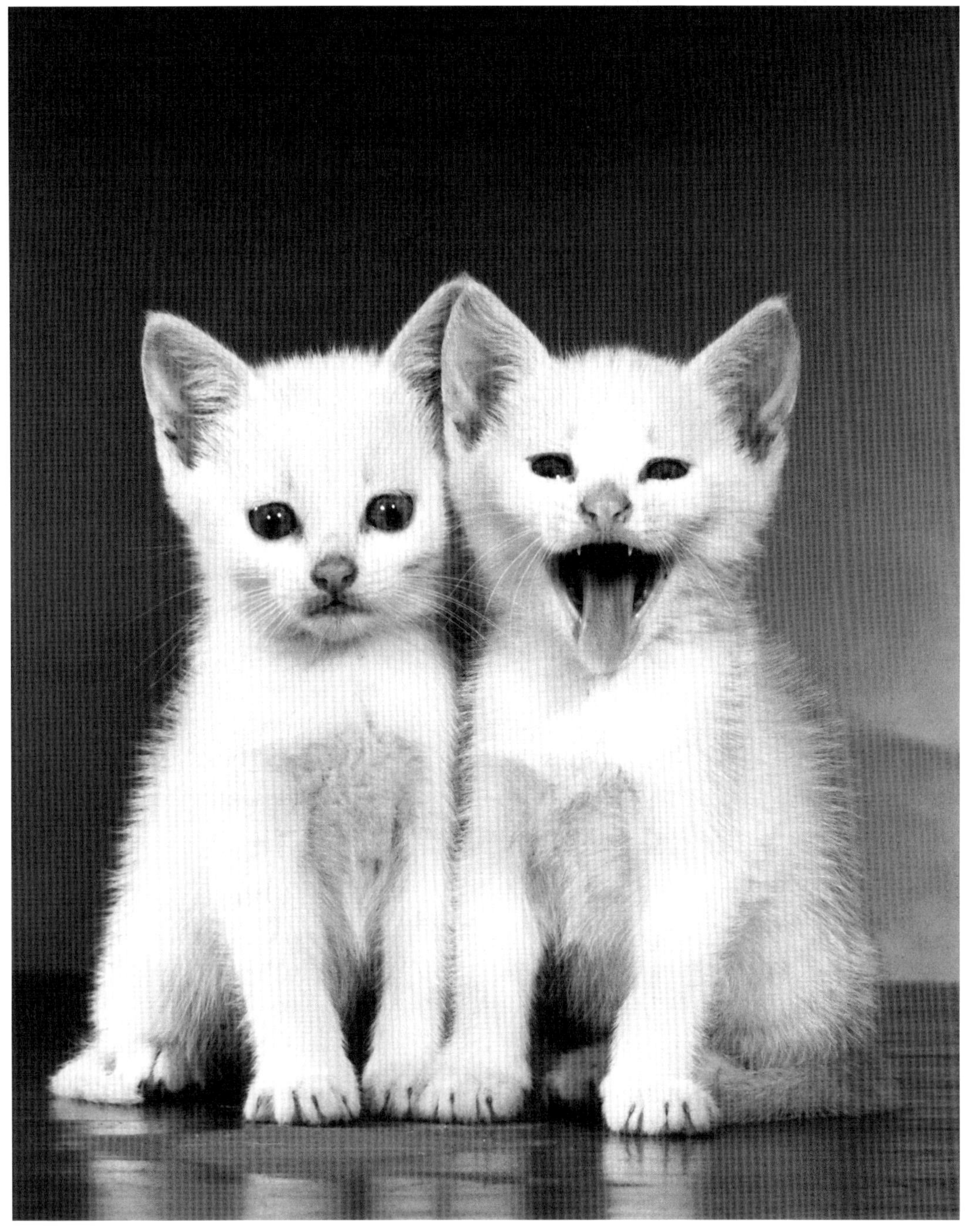

▶LONG ISLAND, 1957

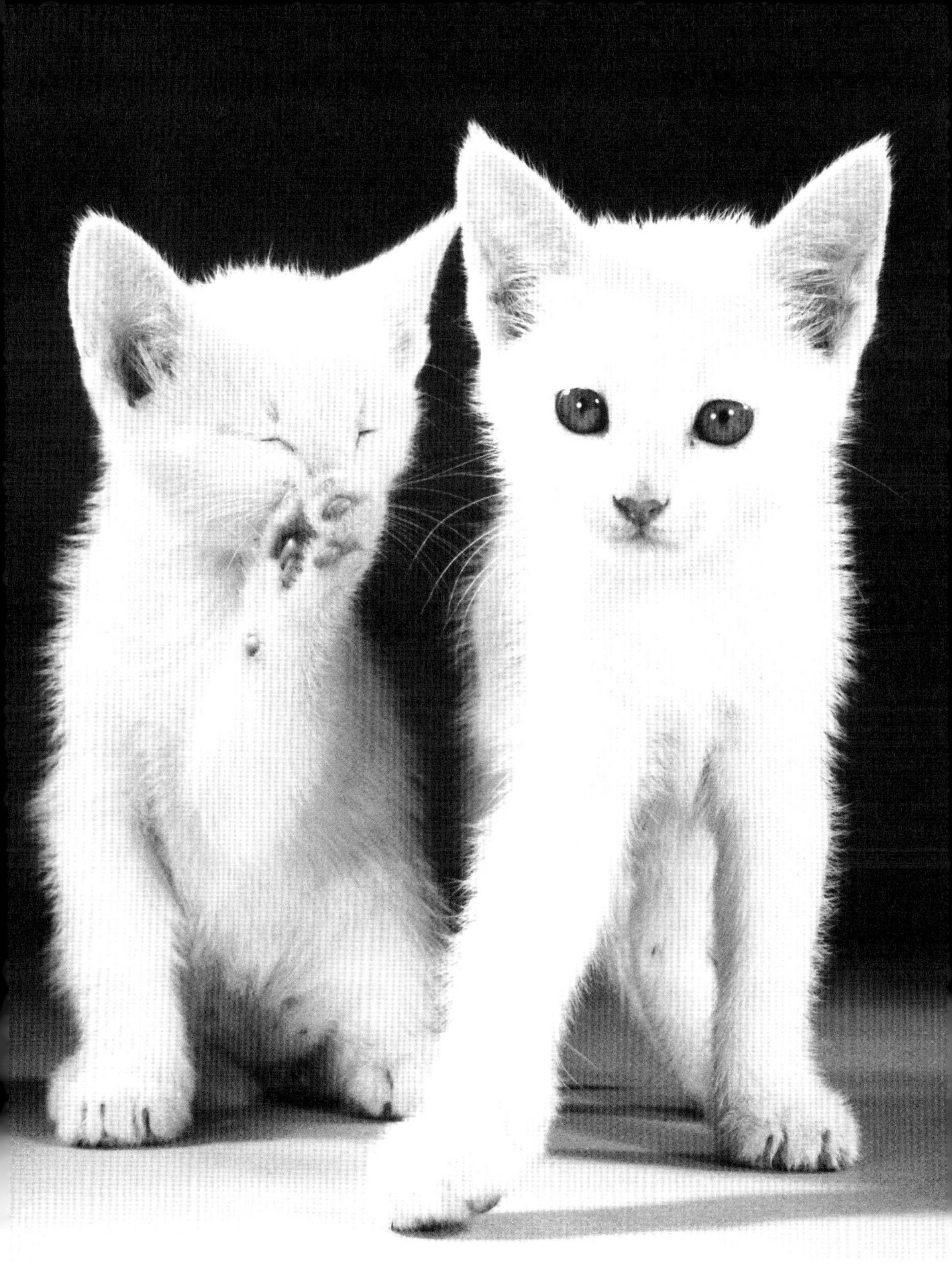

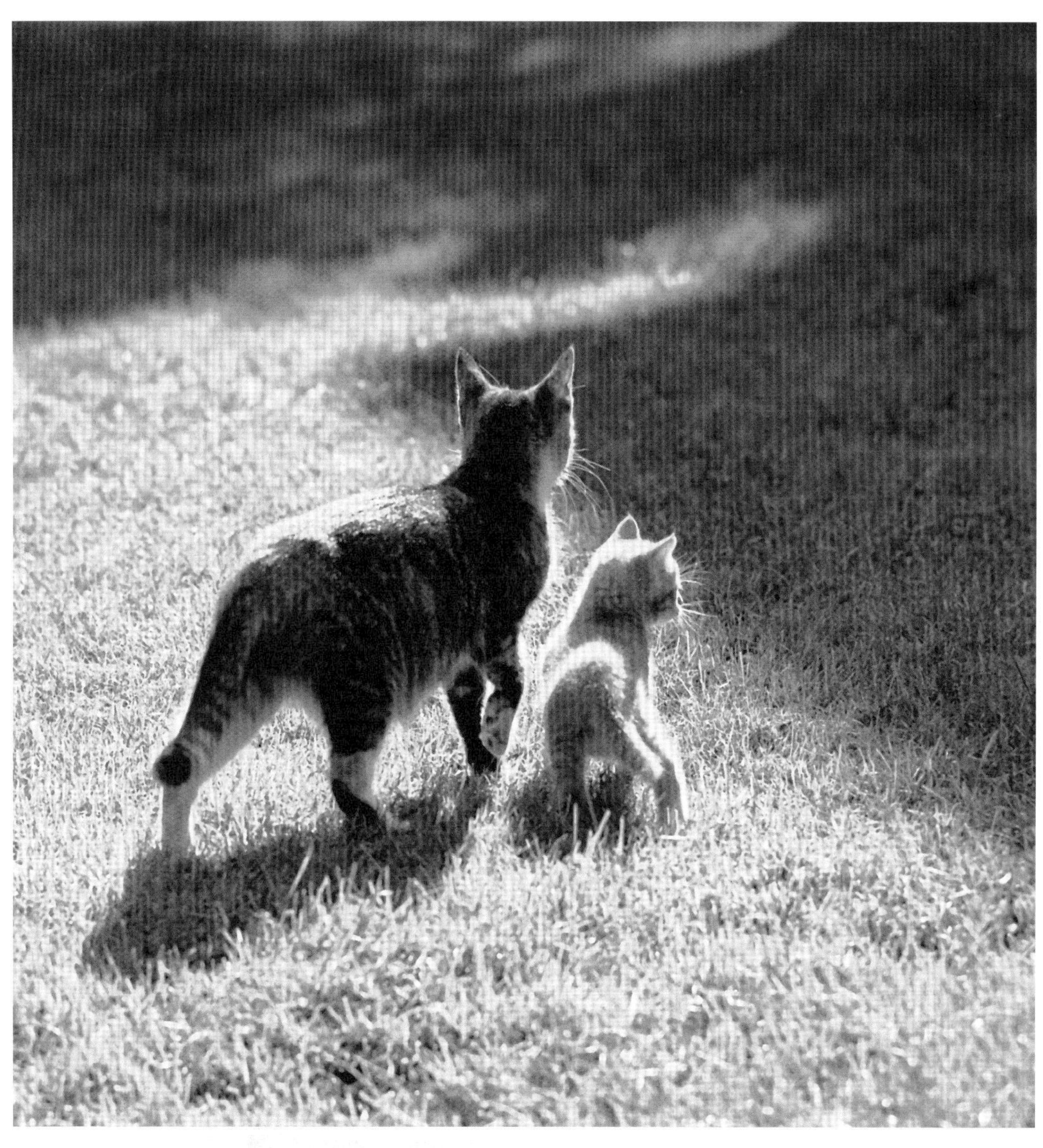

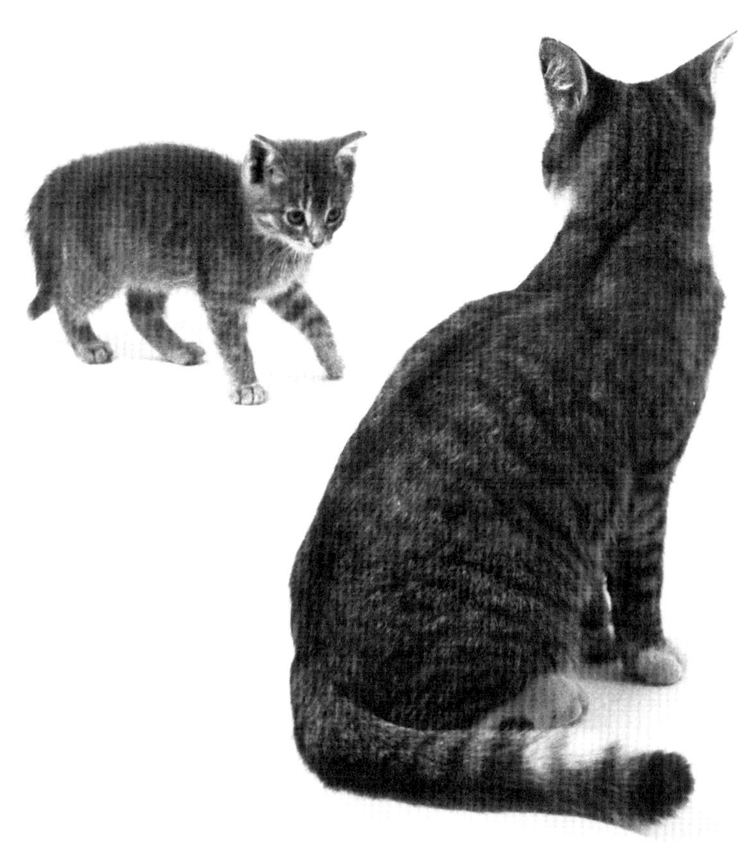

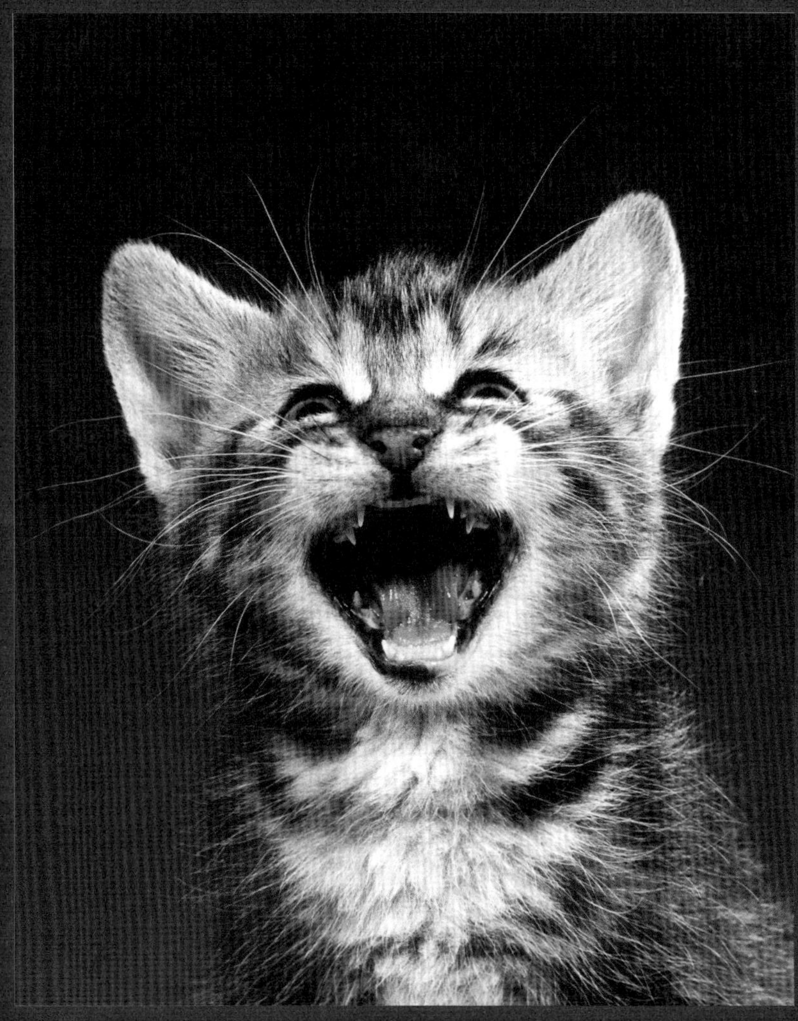

▲LONG ISLAND, 1952

▶LONG ISLAND, 1954

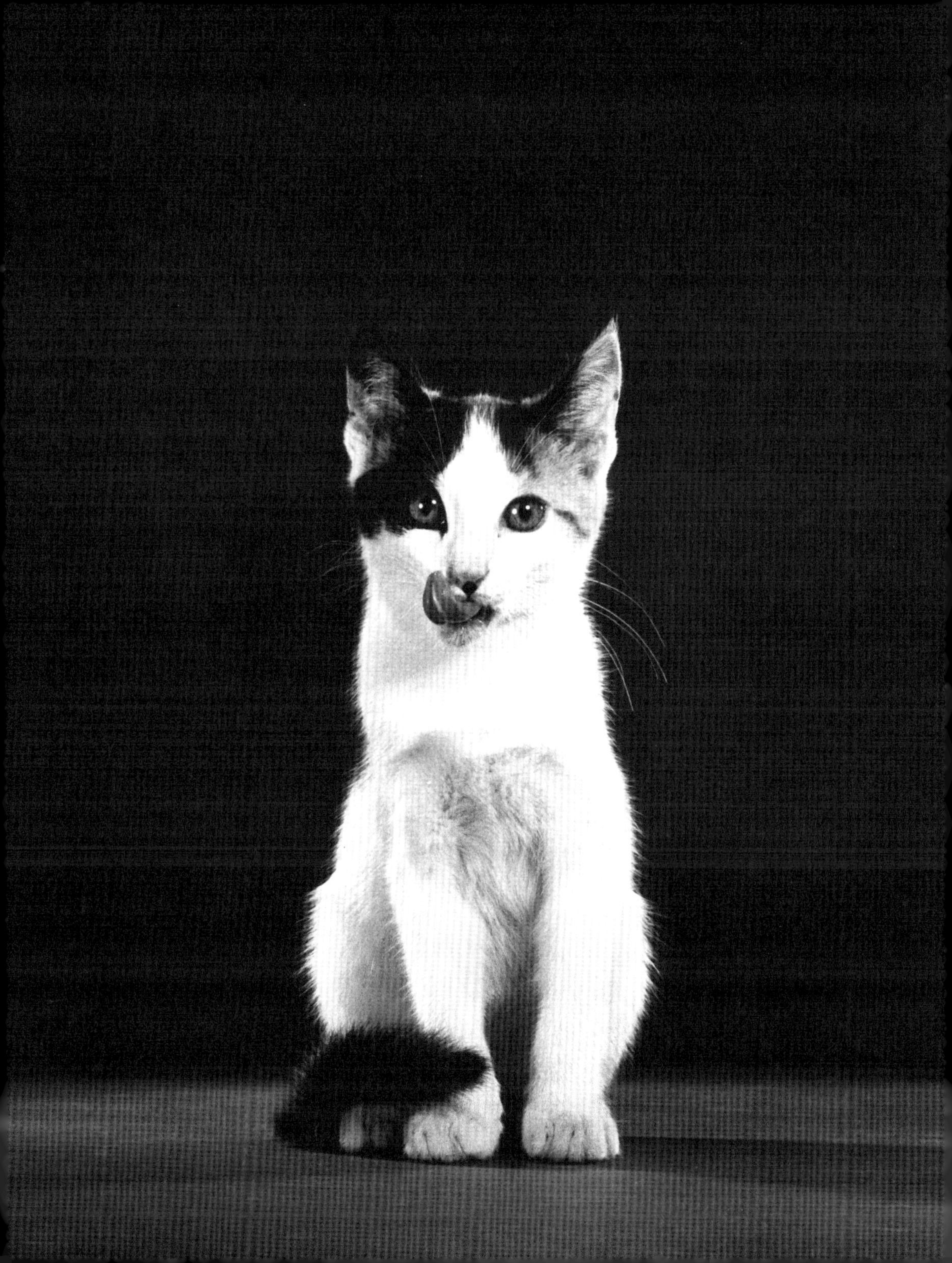

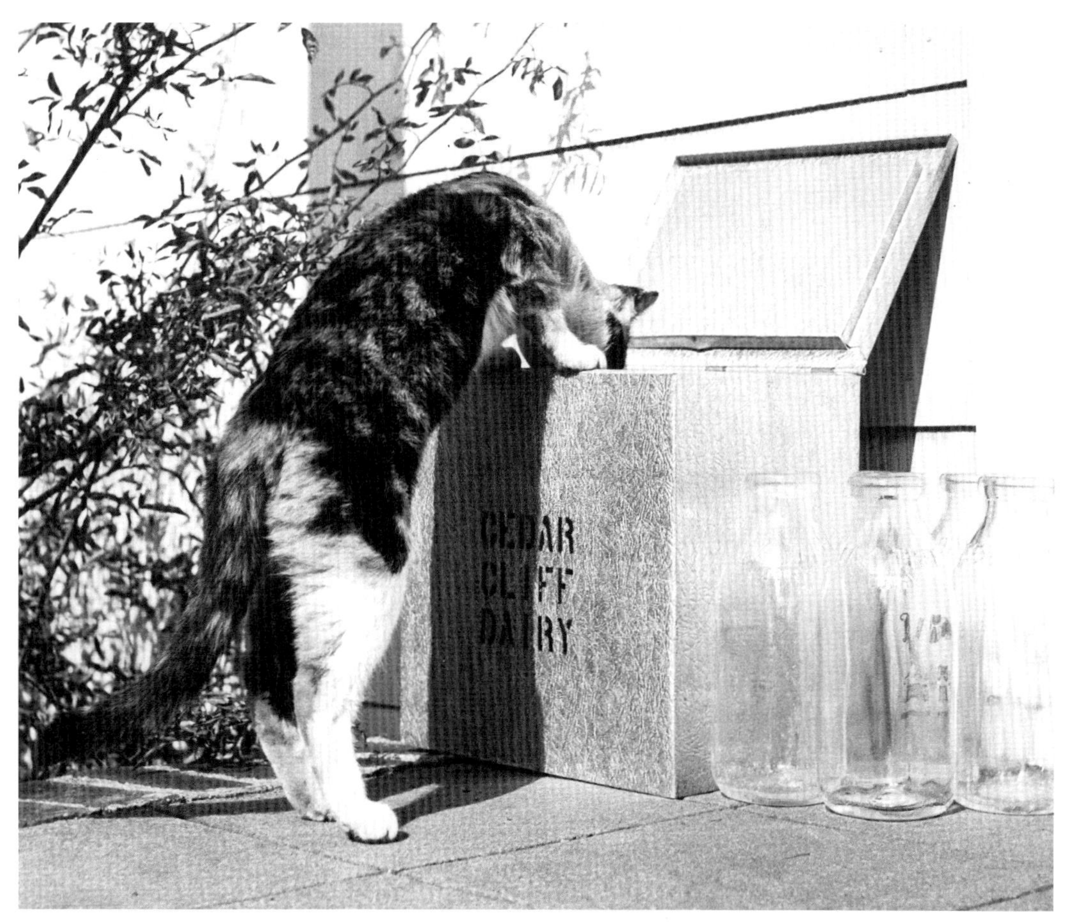

▲LONG ISLAND, 1955   ►LONG ISLAND, 1952

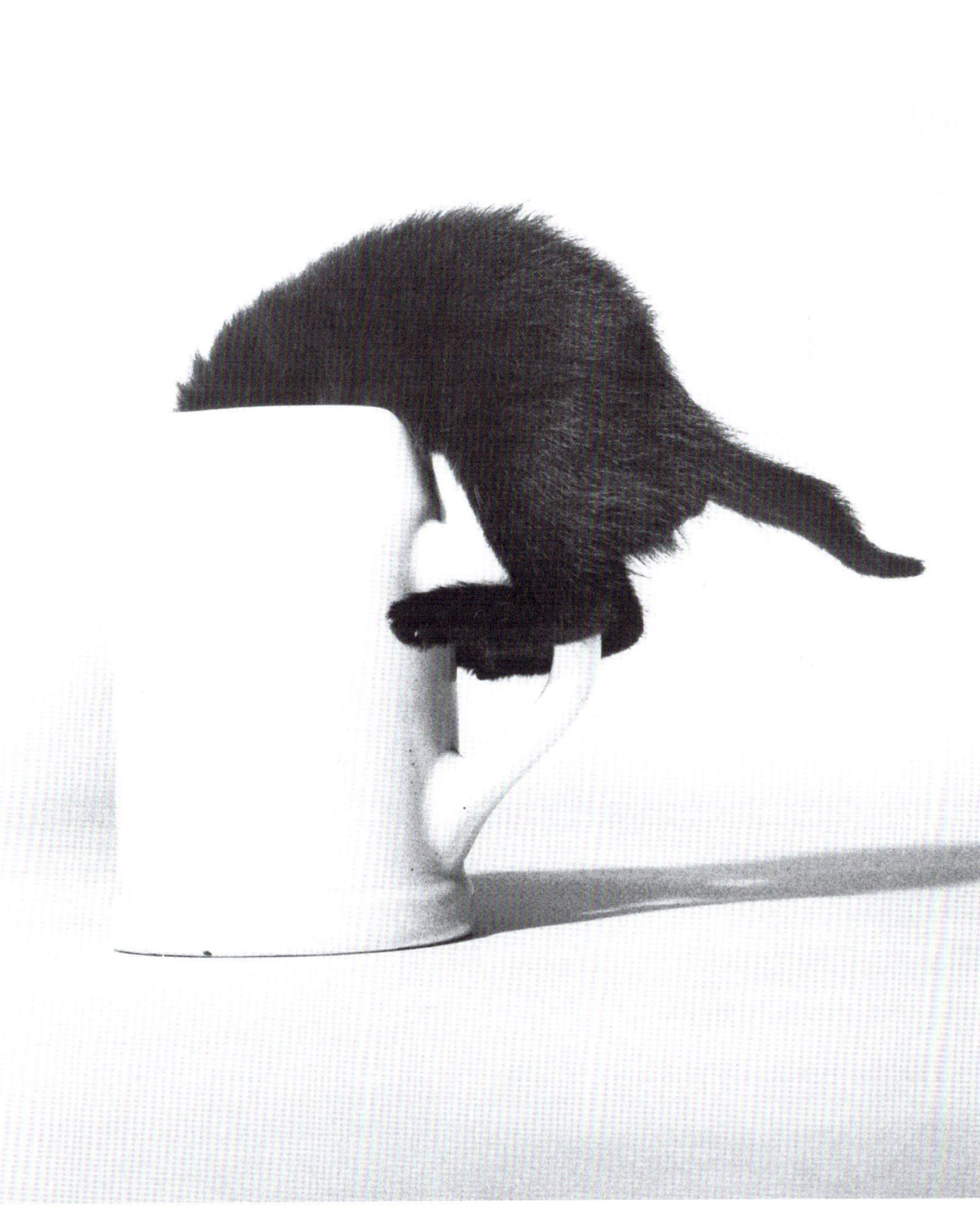

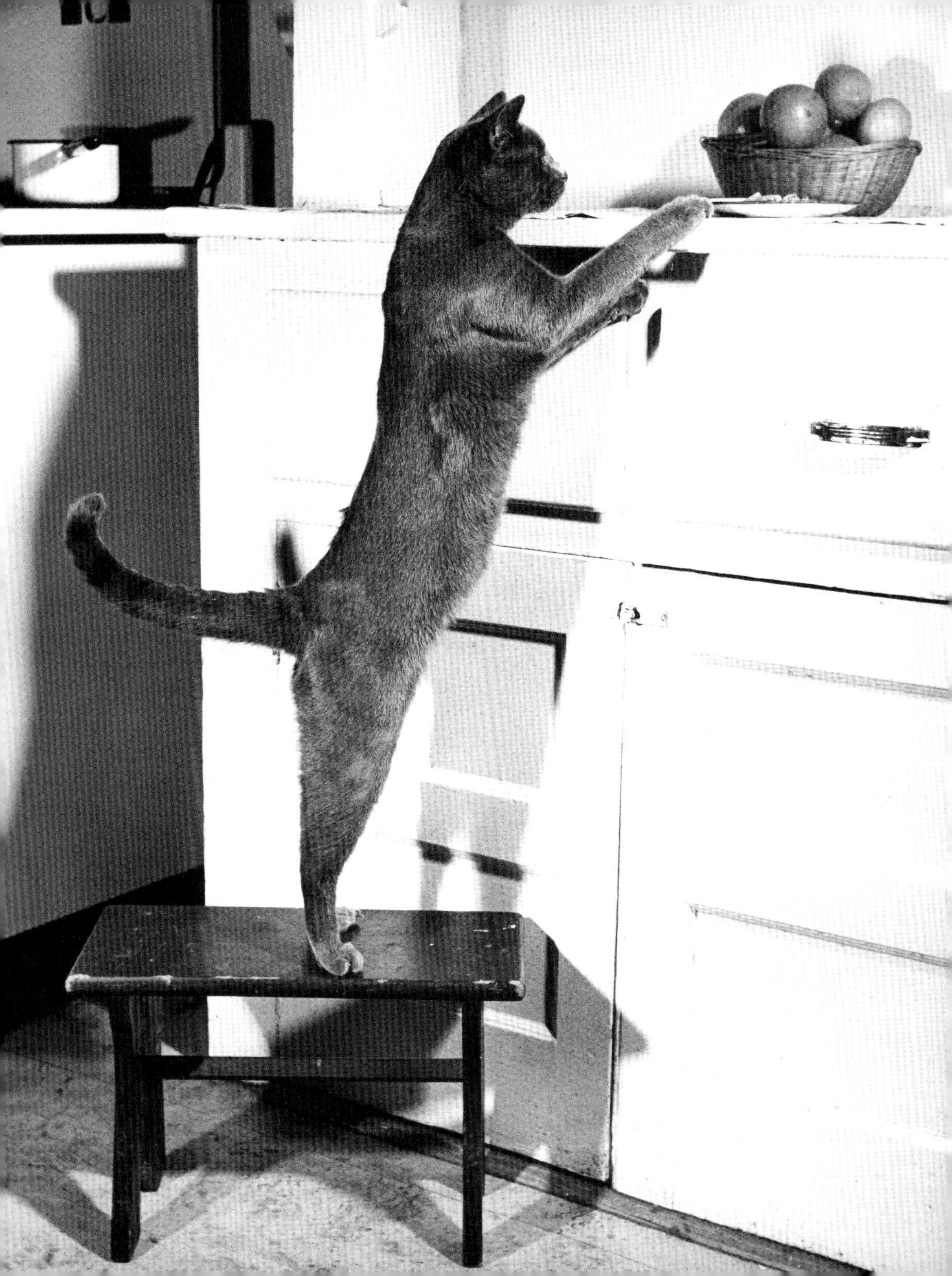

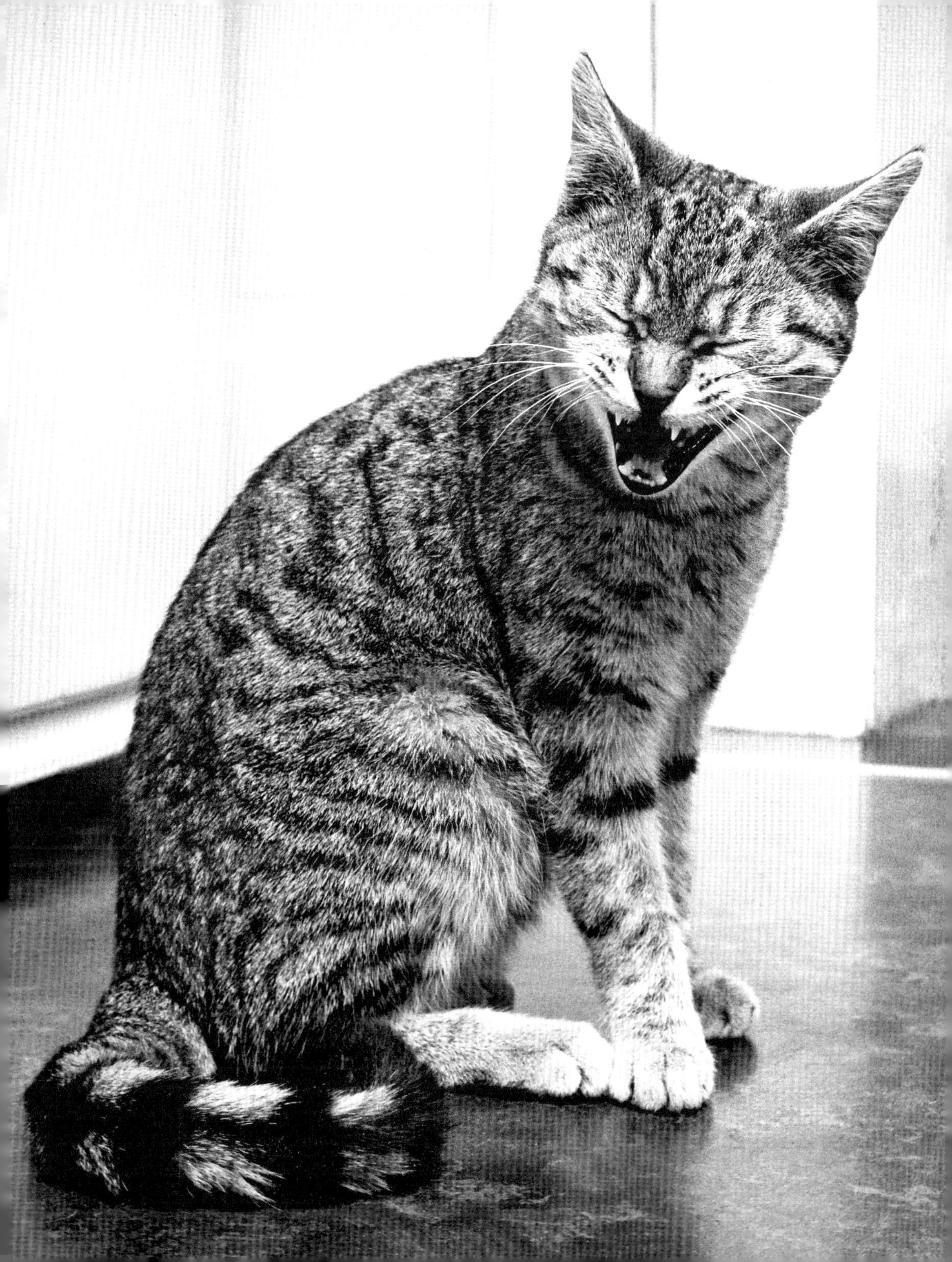

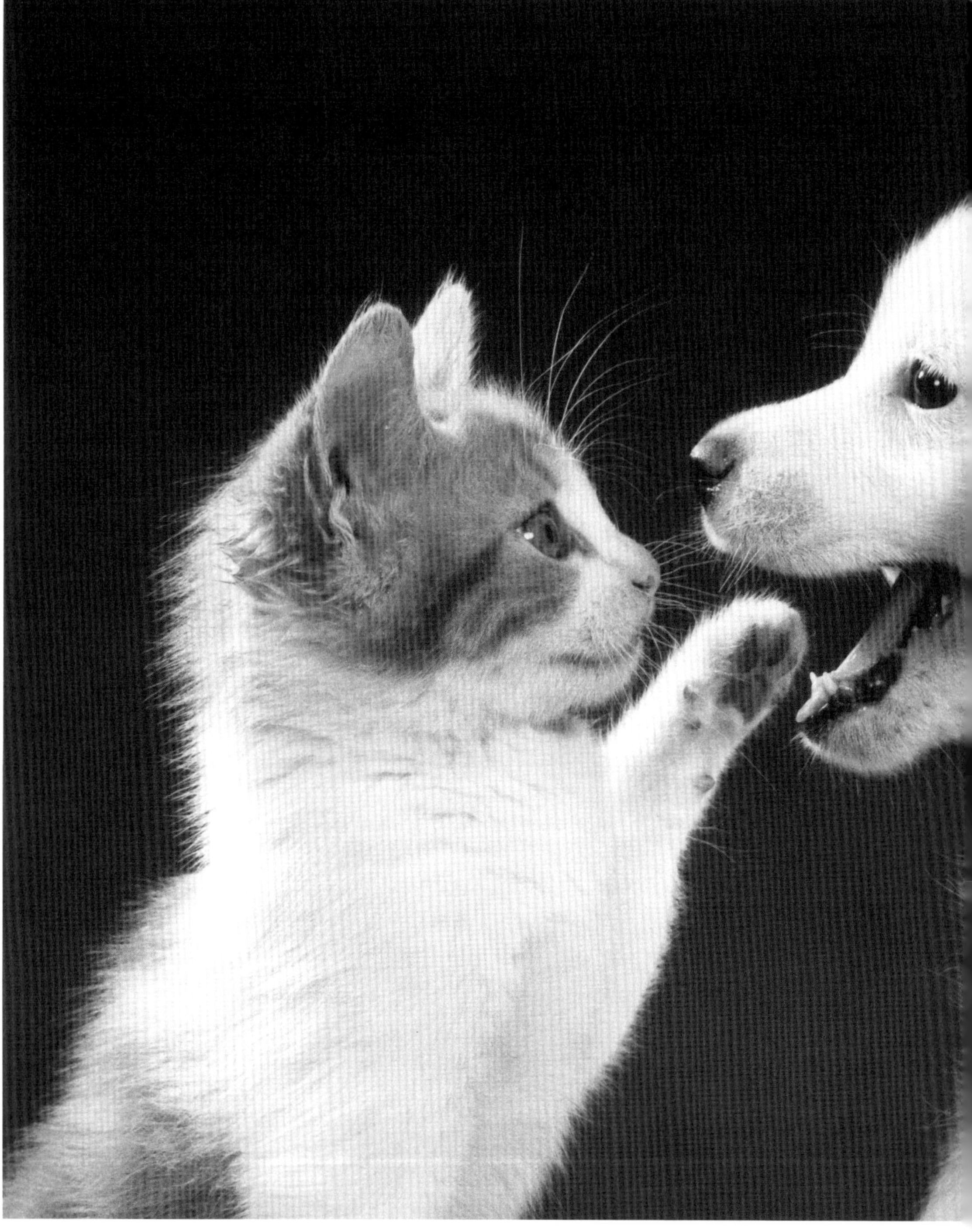

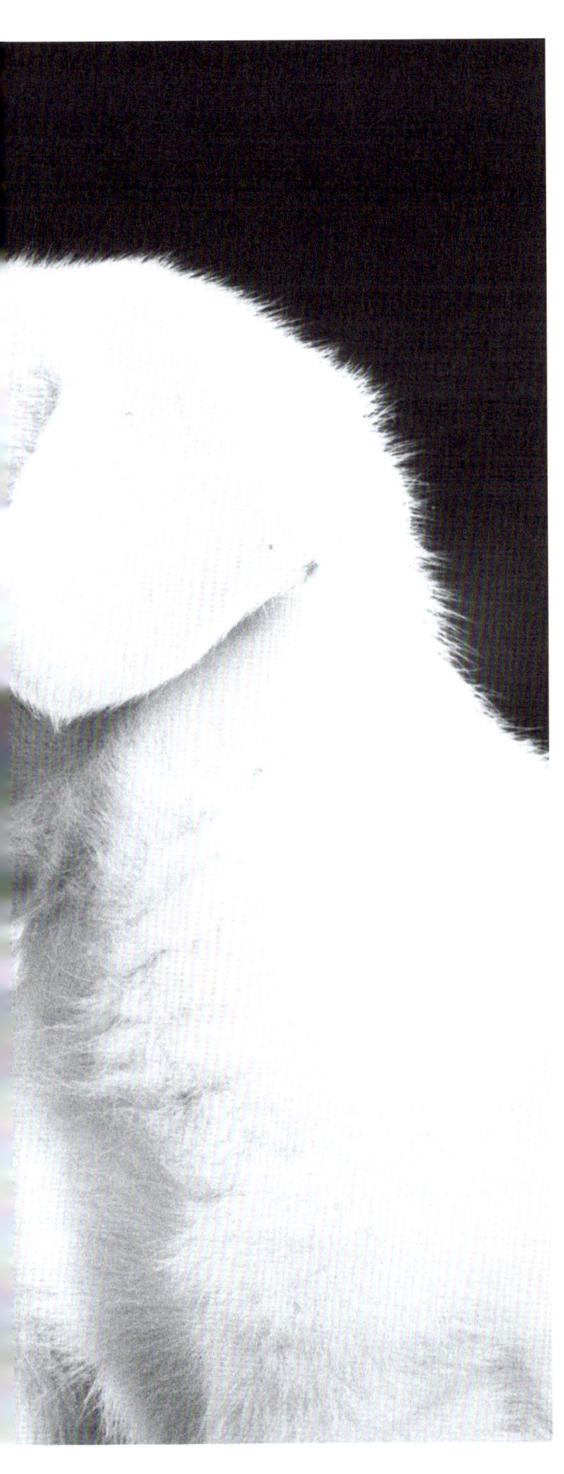

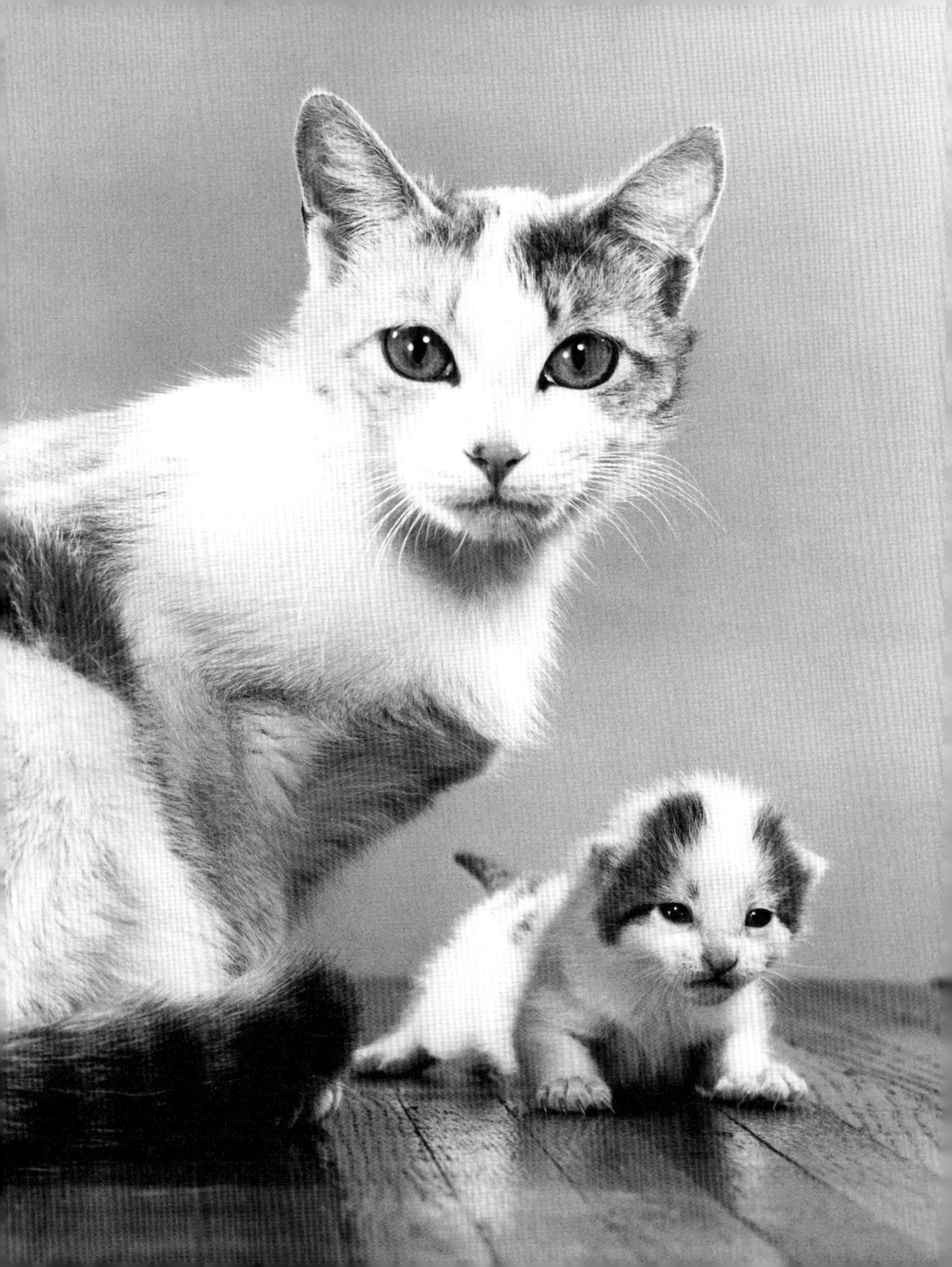

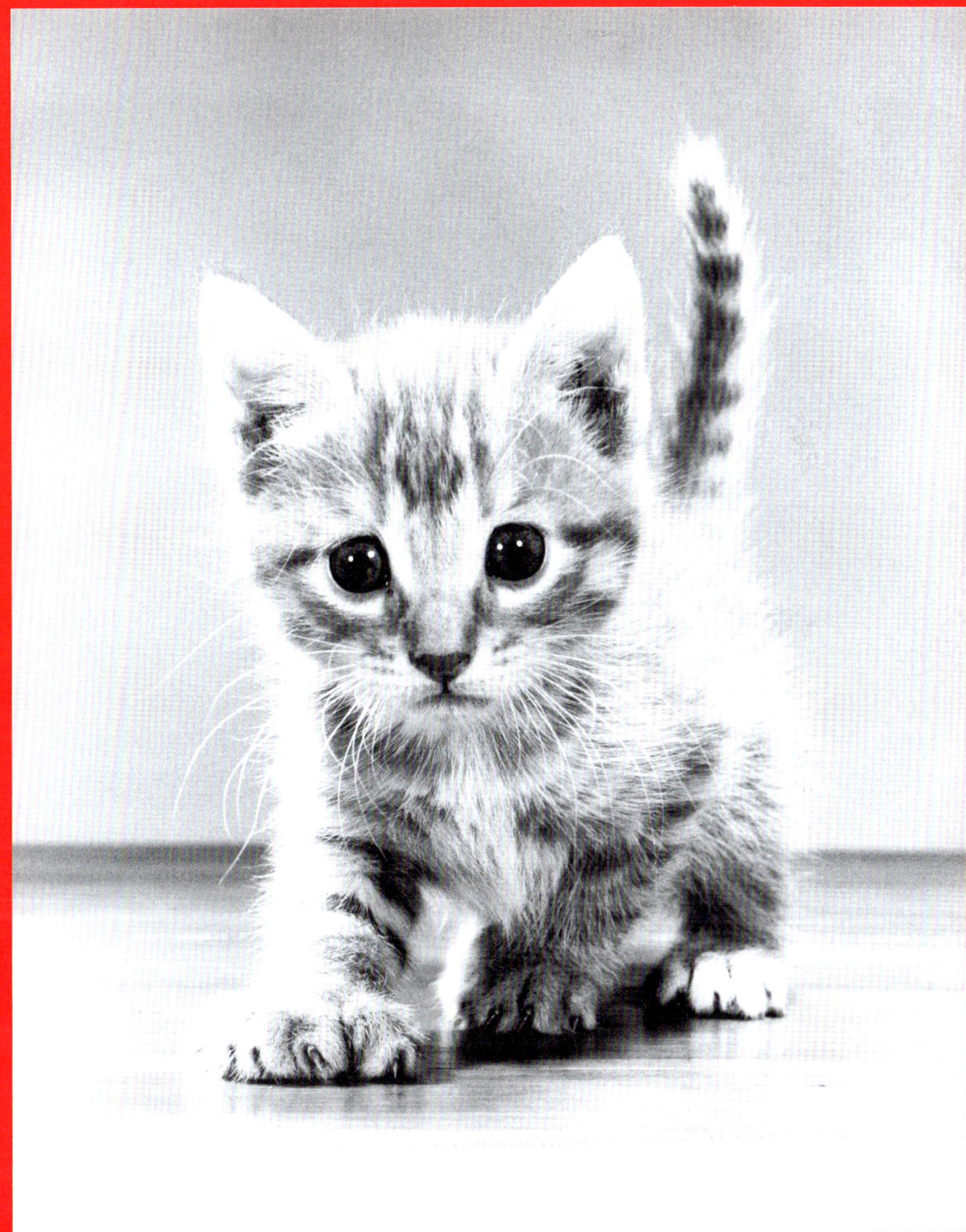

◄ LONG ISLAND, 1956
▲ LONG ISLAND, 1959

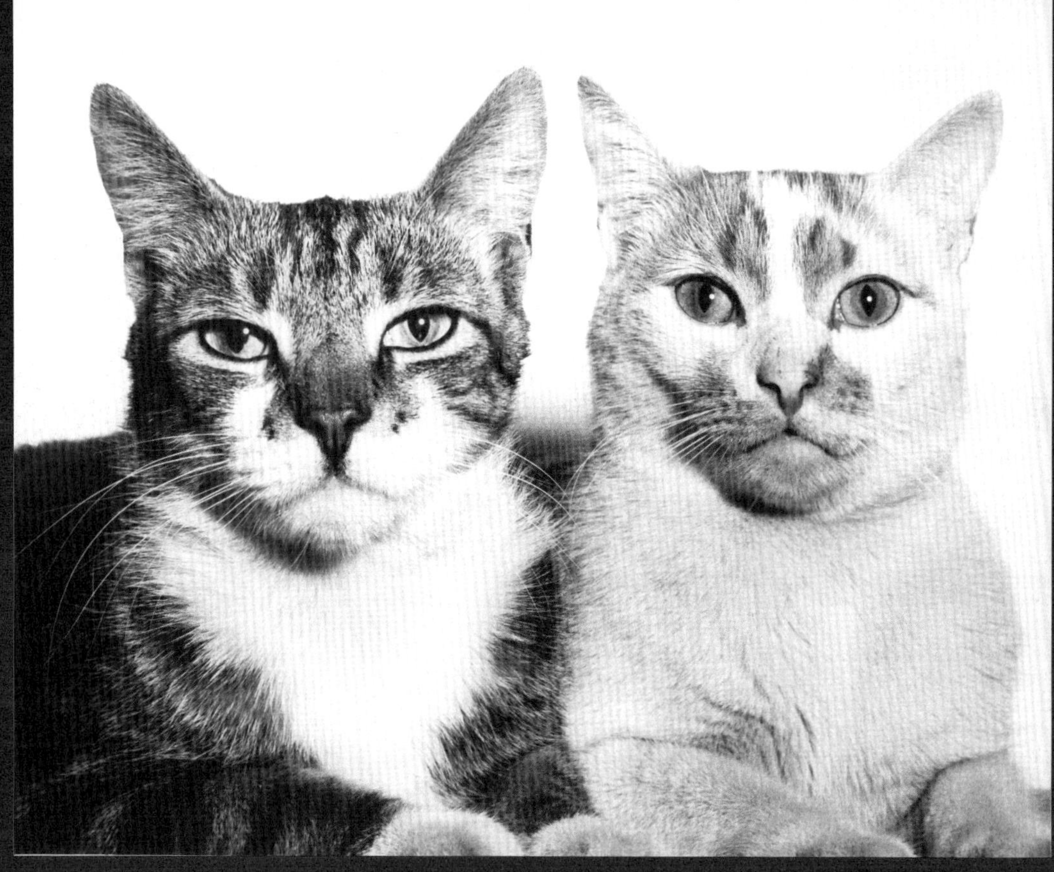

▲LONG ISLAND, 1954

►NEW JERSEY, 1962

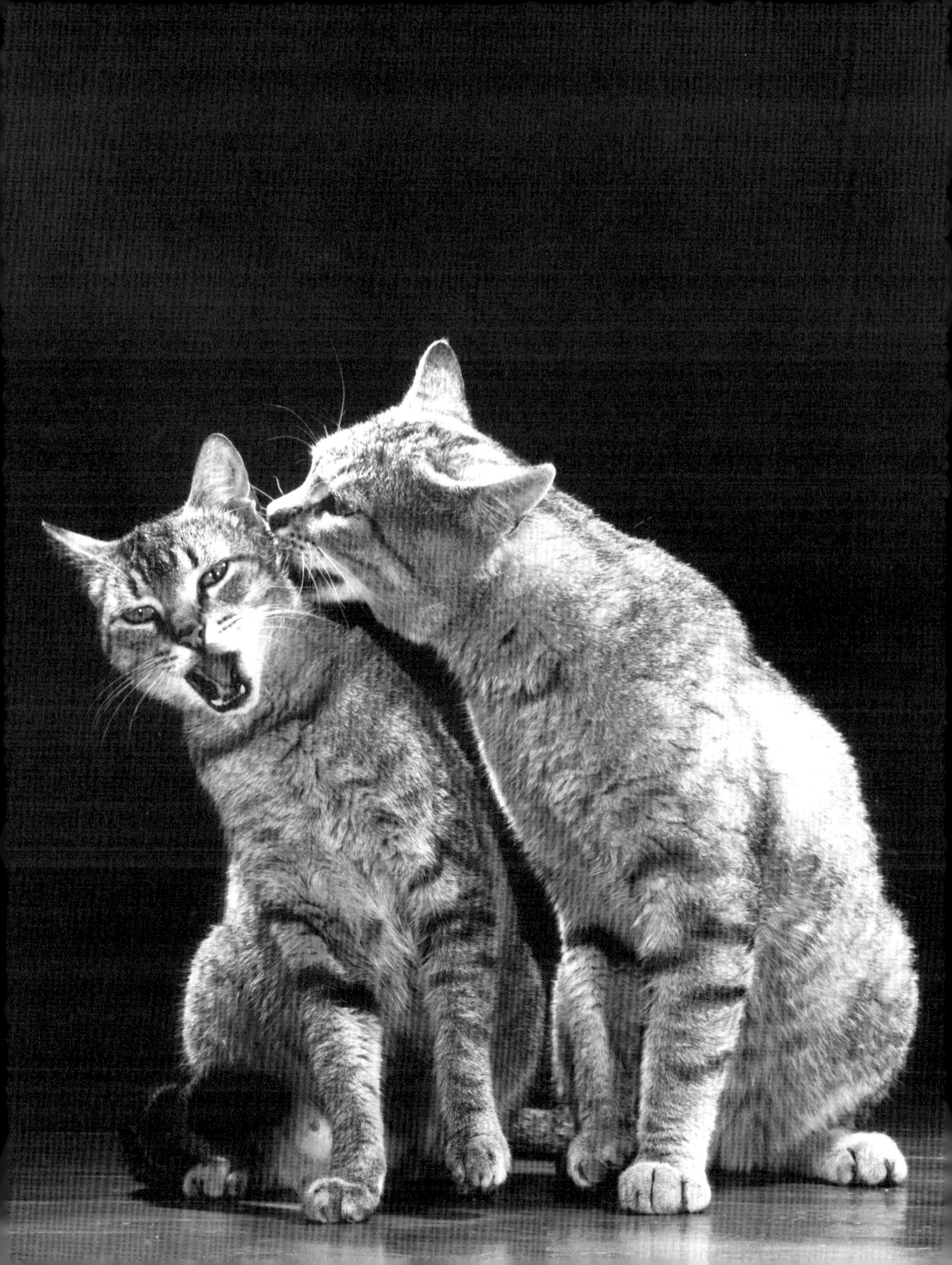

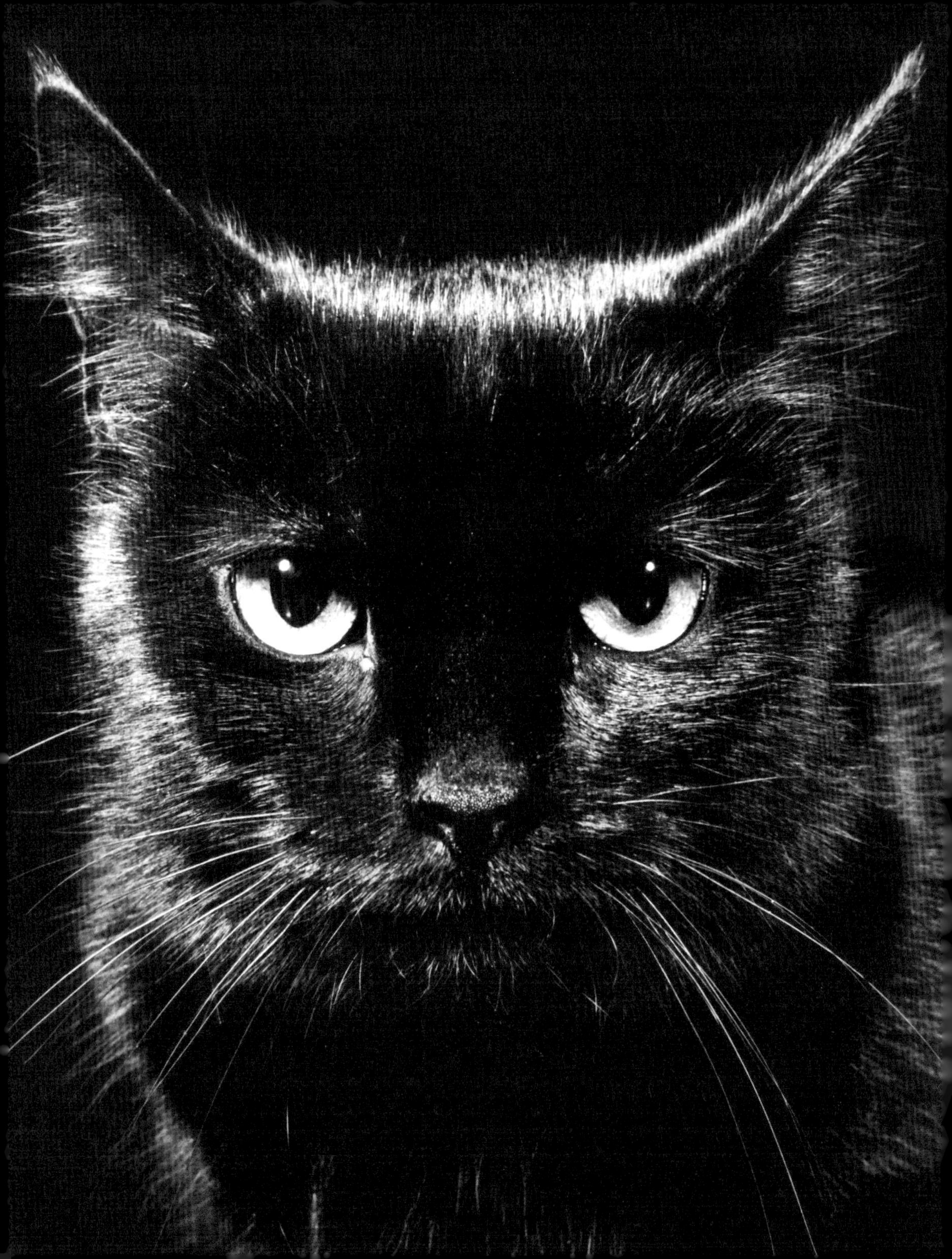

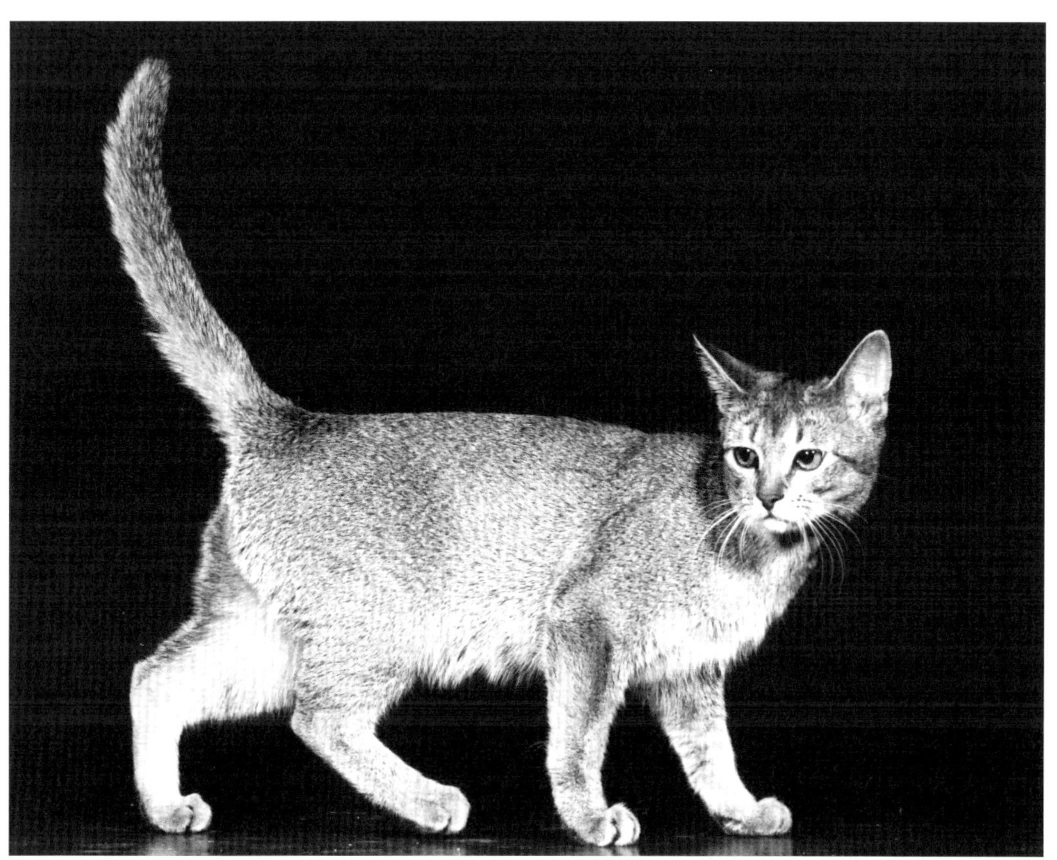

◀ LONG ISLAND, 1952

▲ NEW YORK CITY, 1950

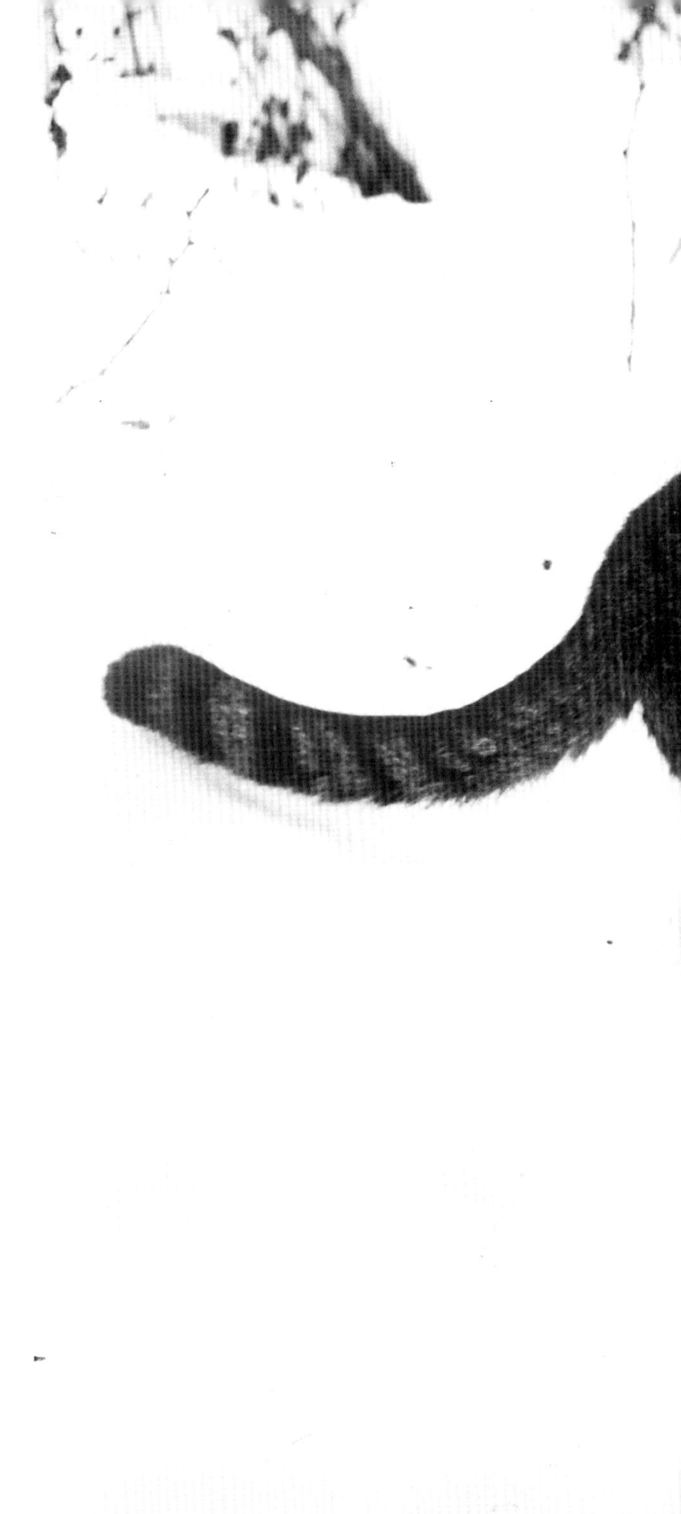

NEW JERSEY, 1960

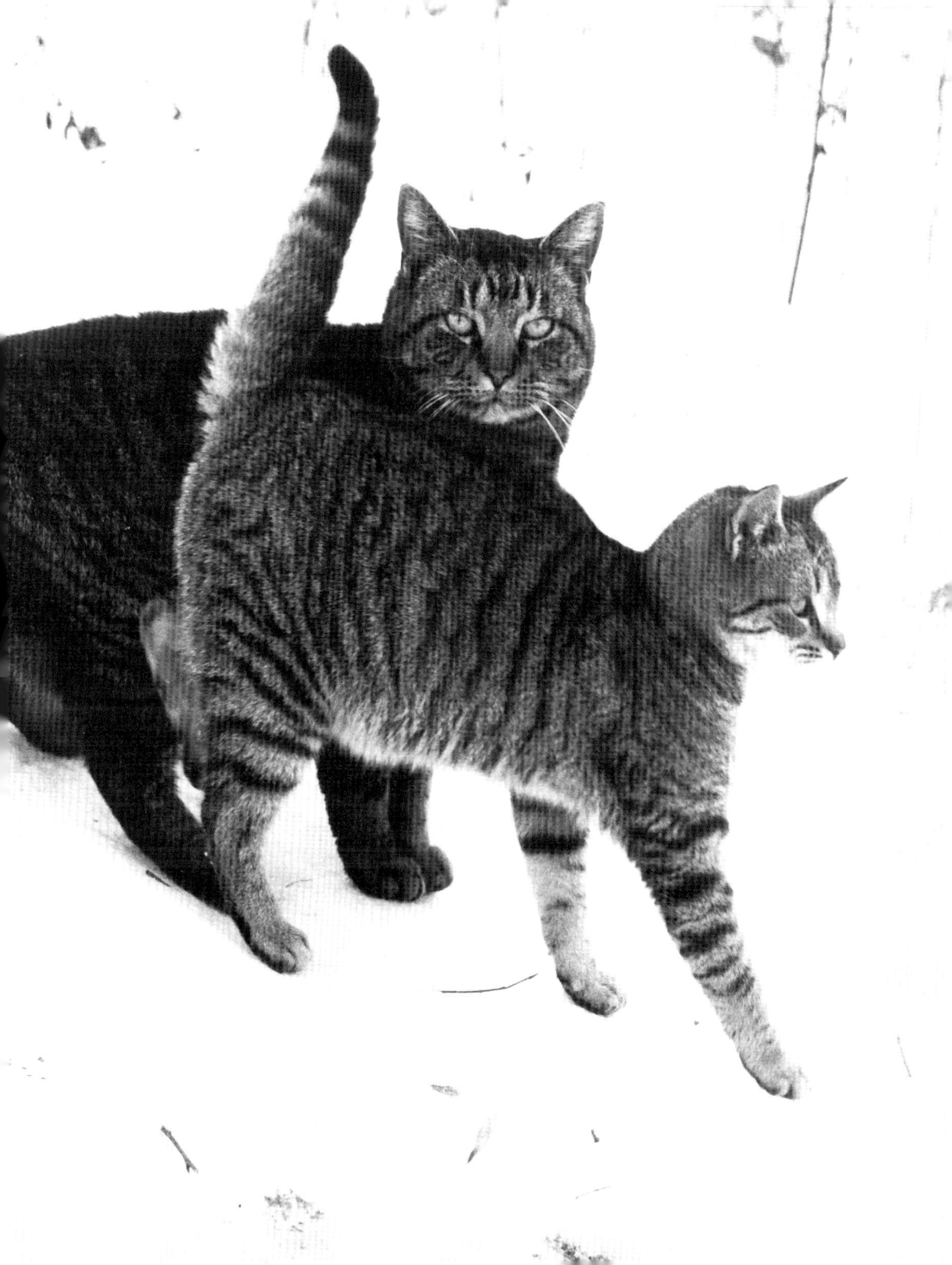

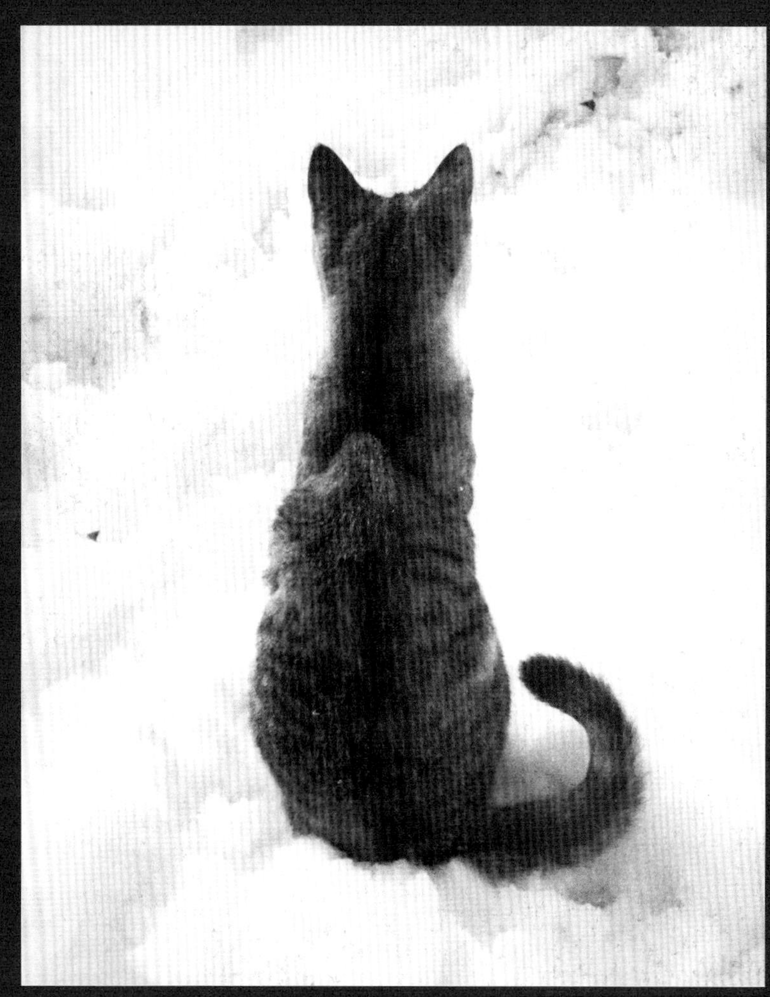

▲LONG ISLAND, 1958

►NEW JERSEY, 1962

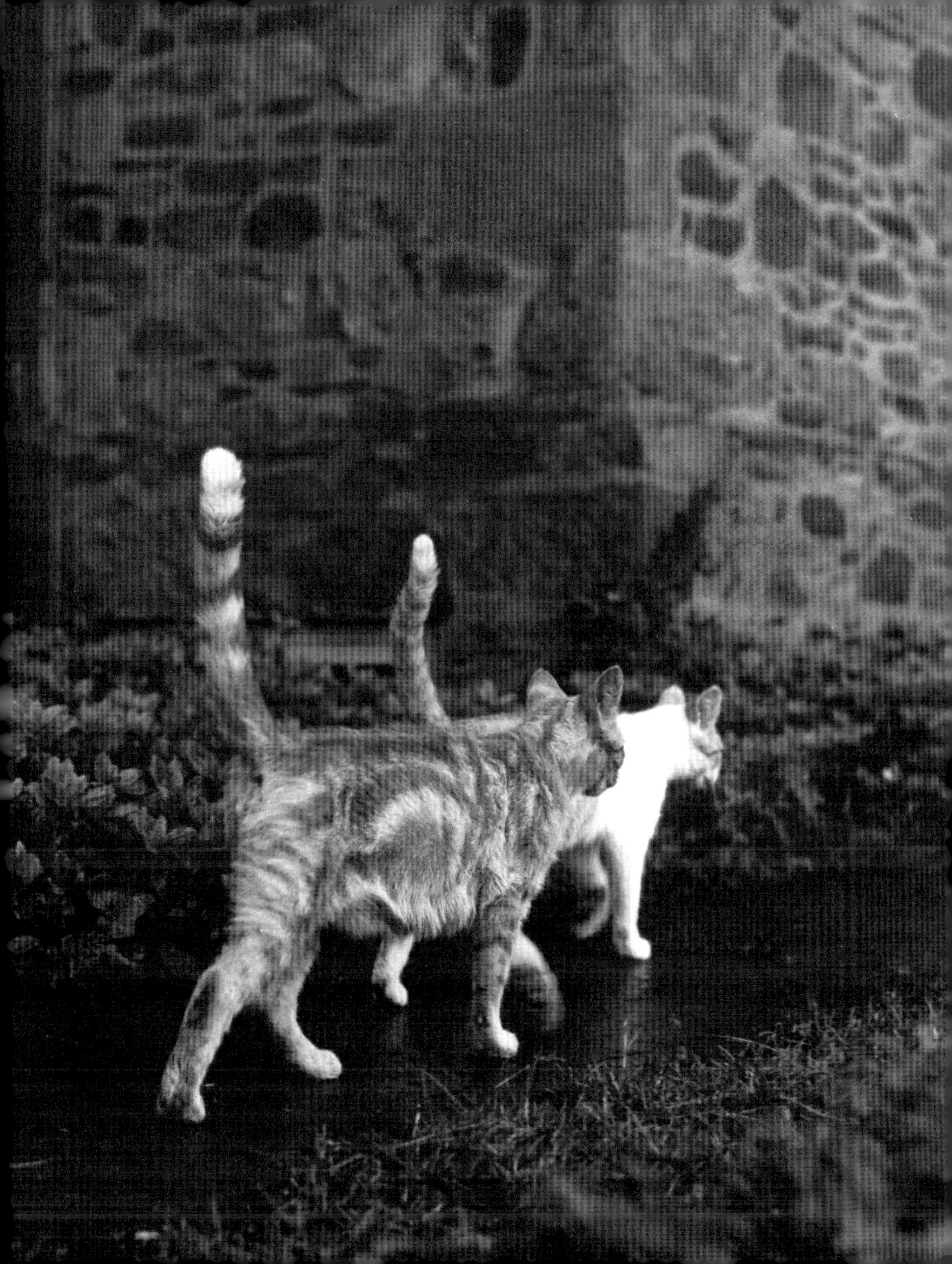

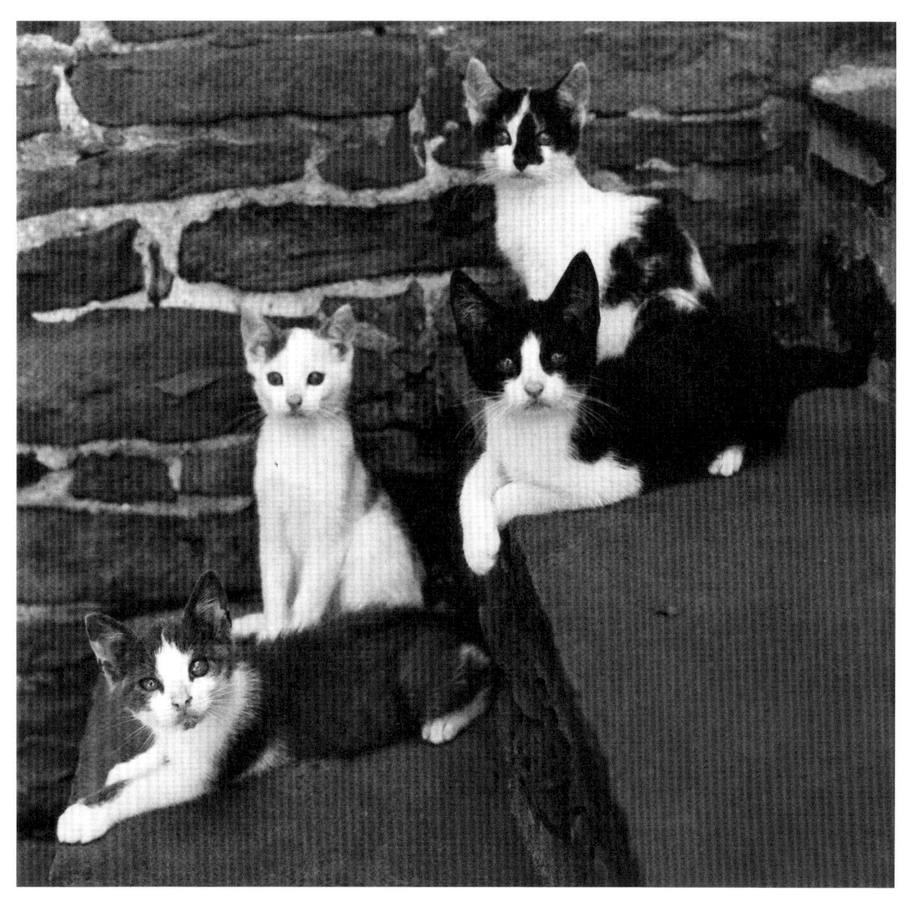

▶NEW JERSEY, 1961

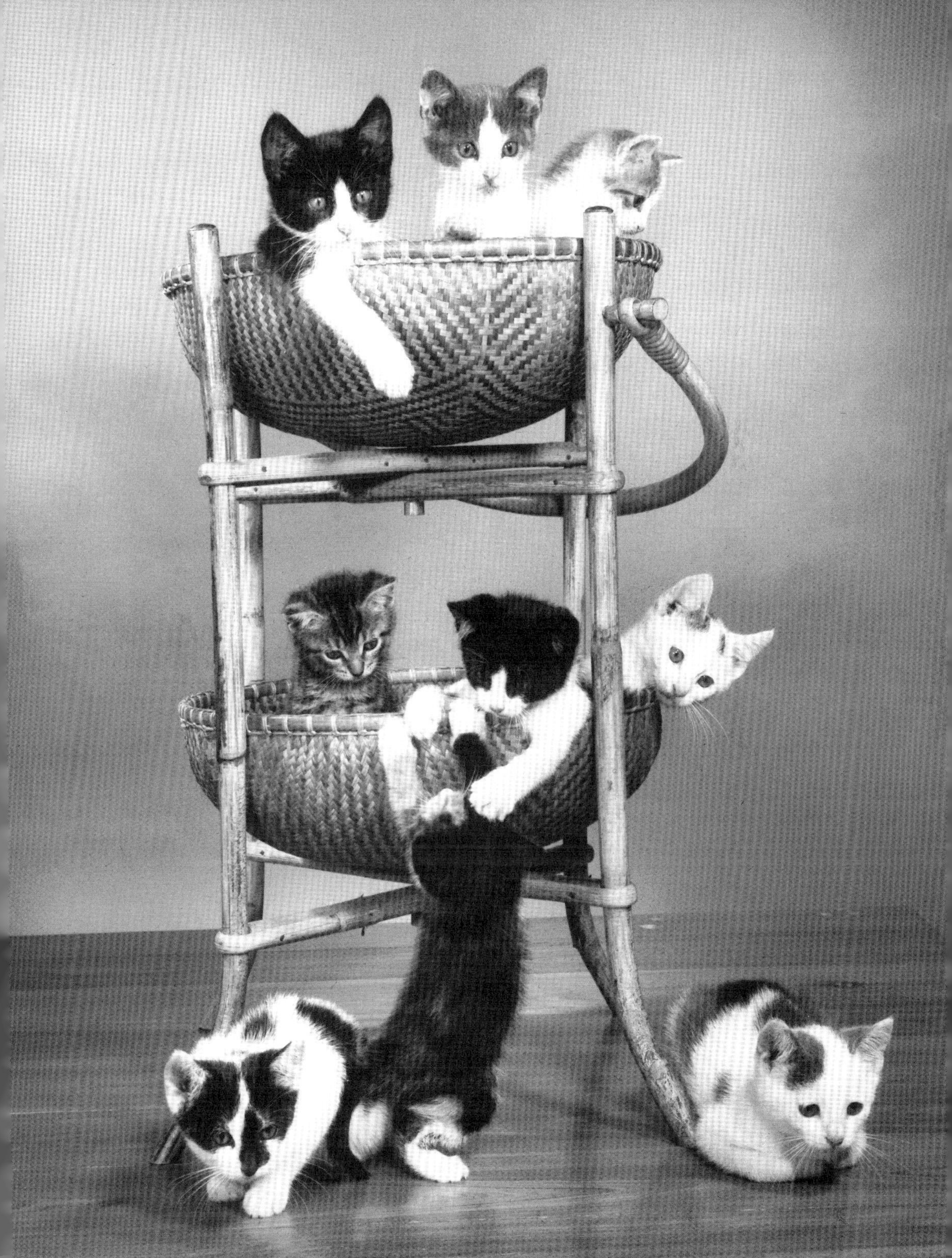

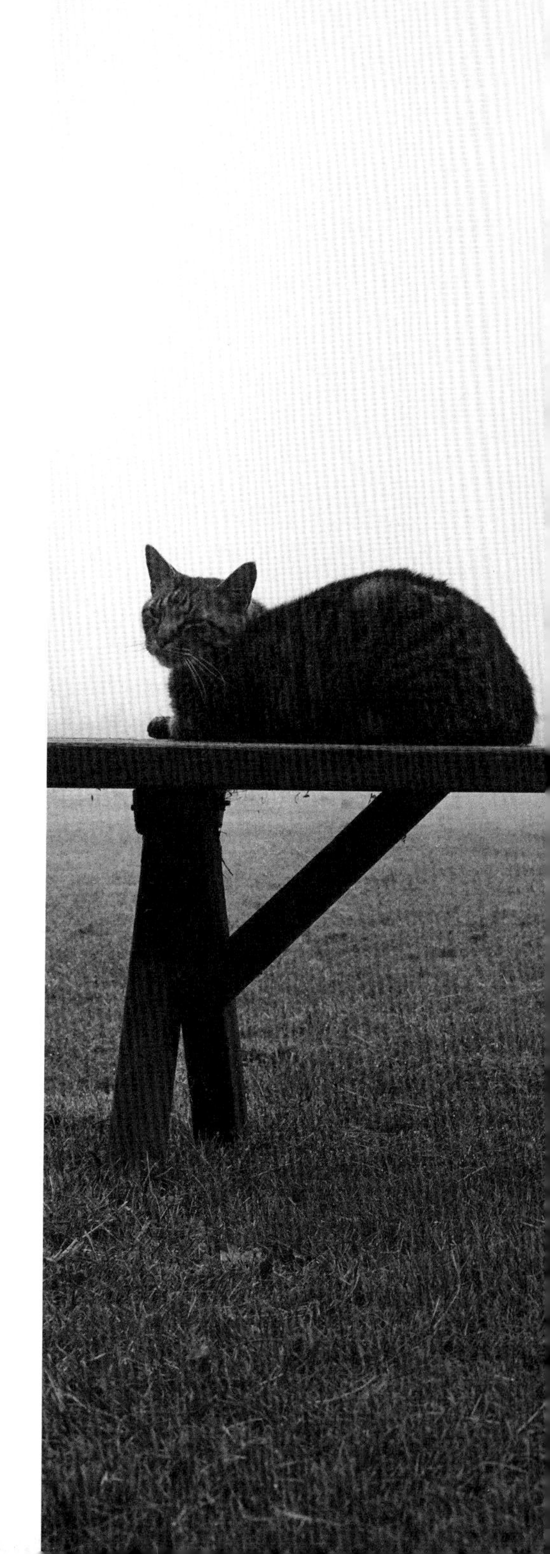

NEW JERSEY, 1961

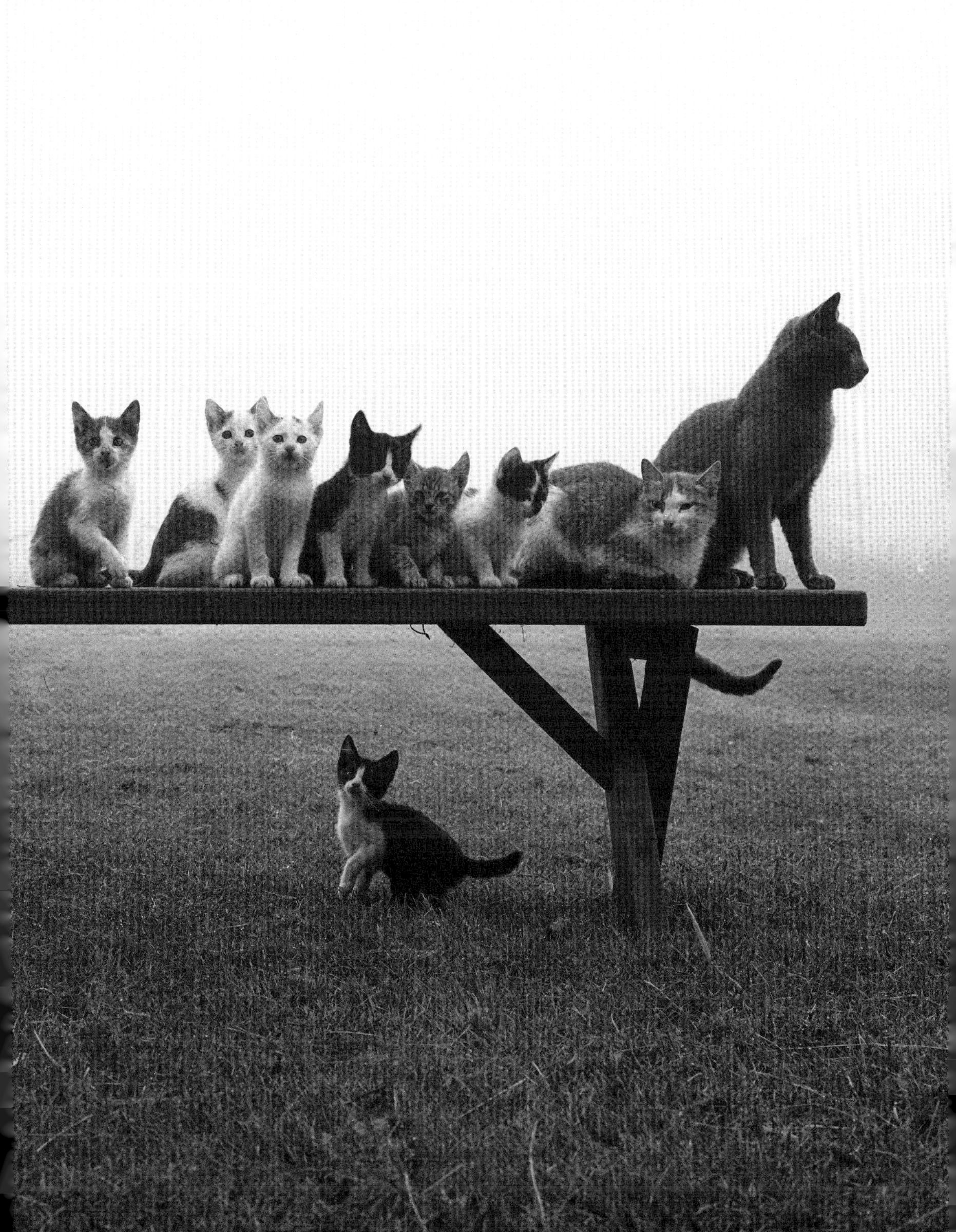

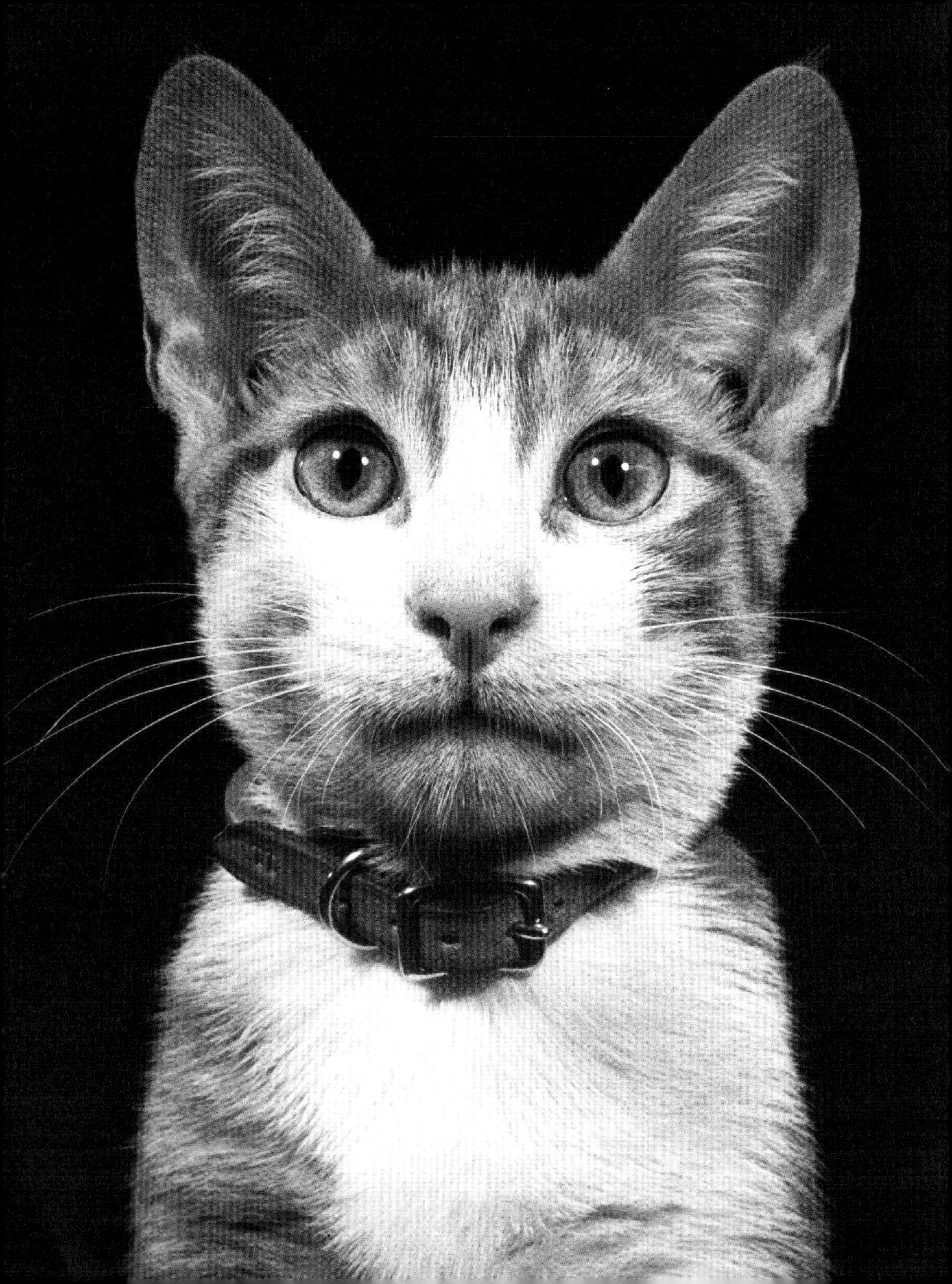

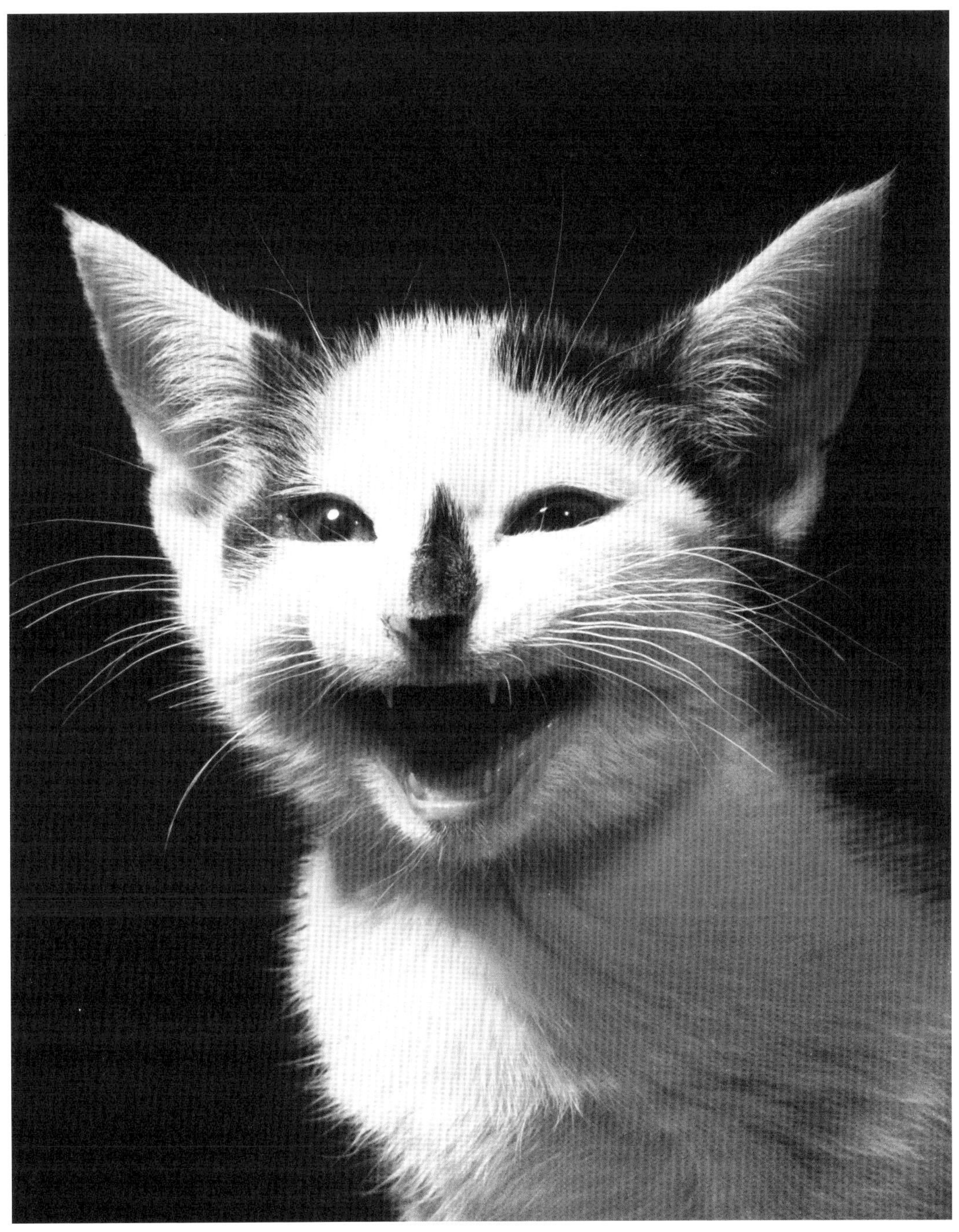

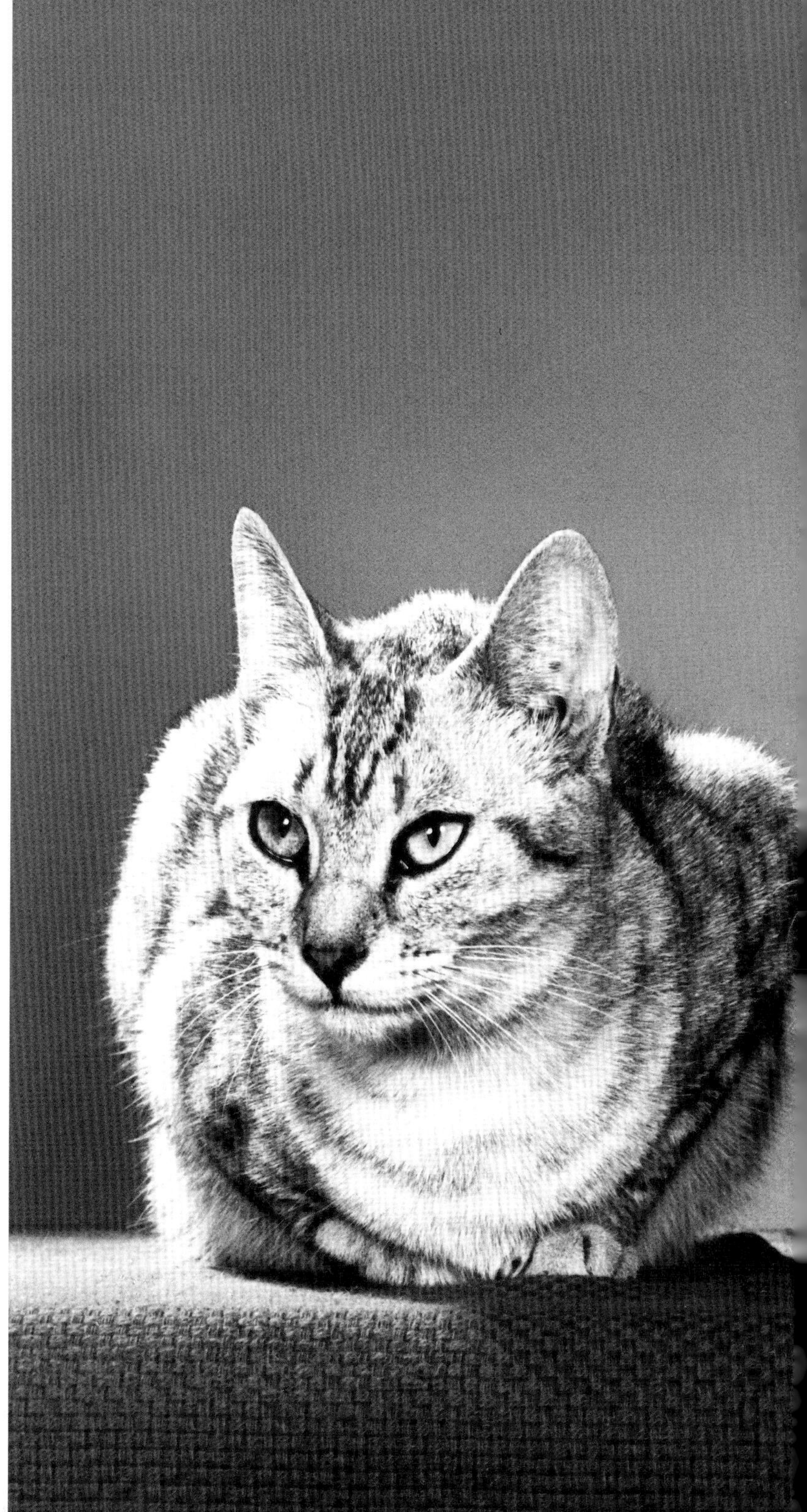

LONG ISLAND, 1955

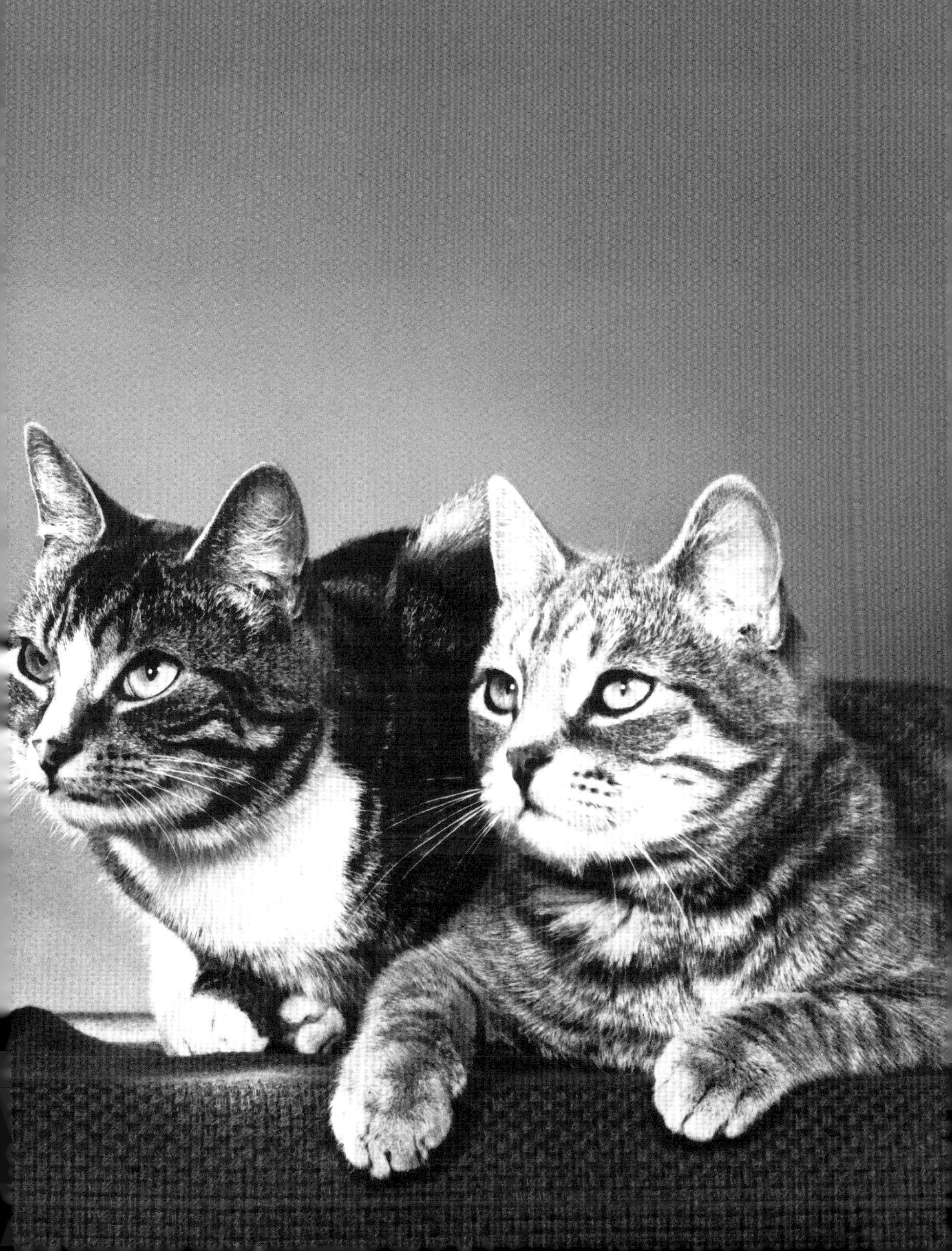

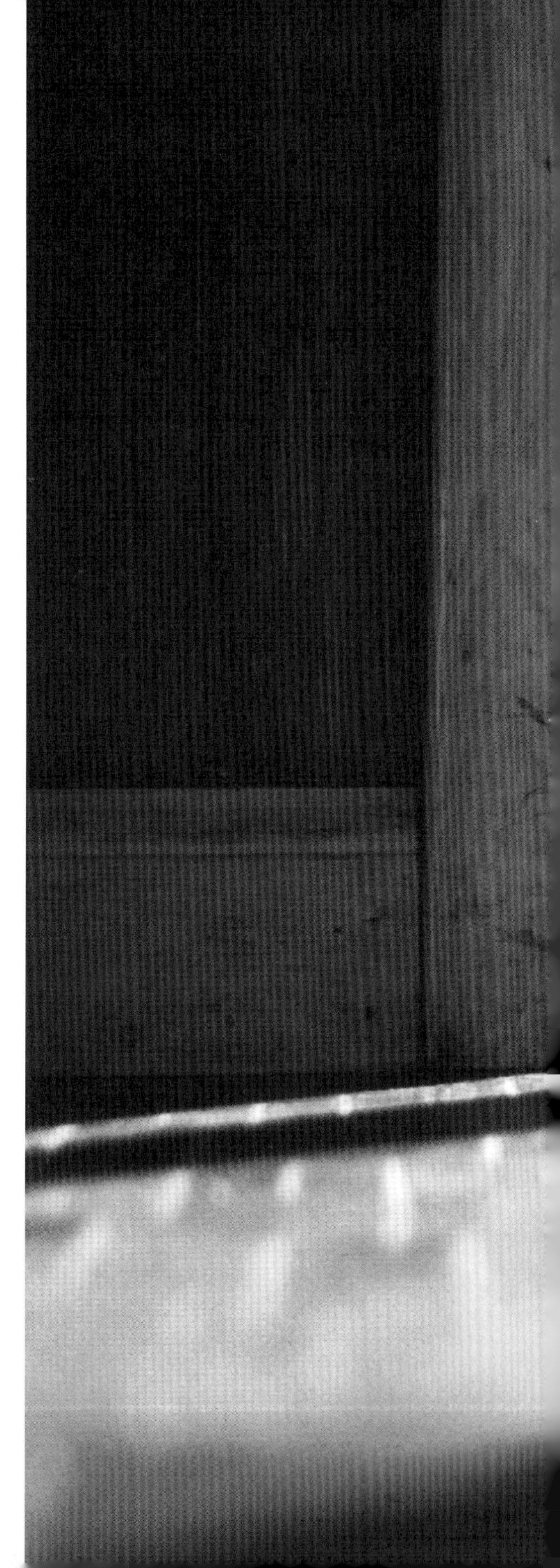

LONG ISLAND, 1958

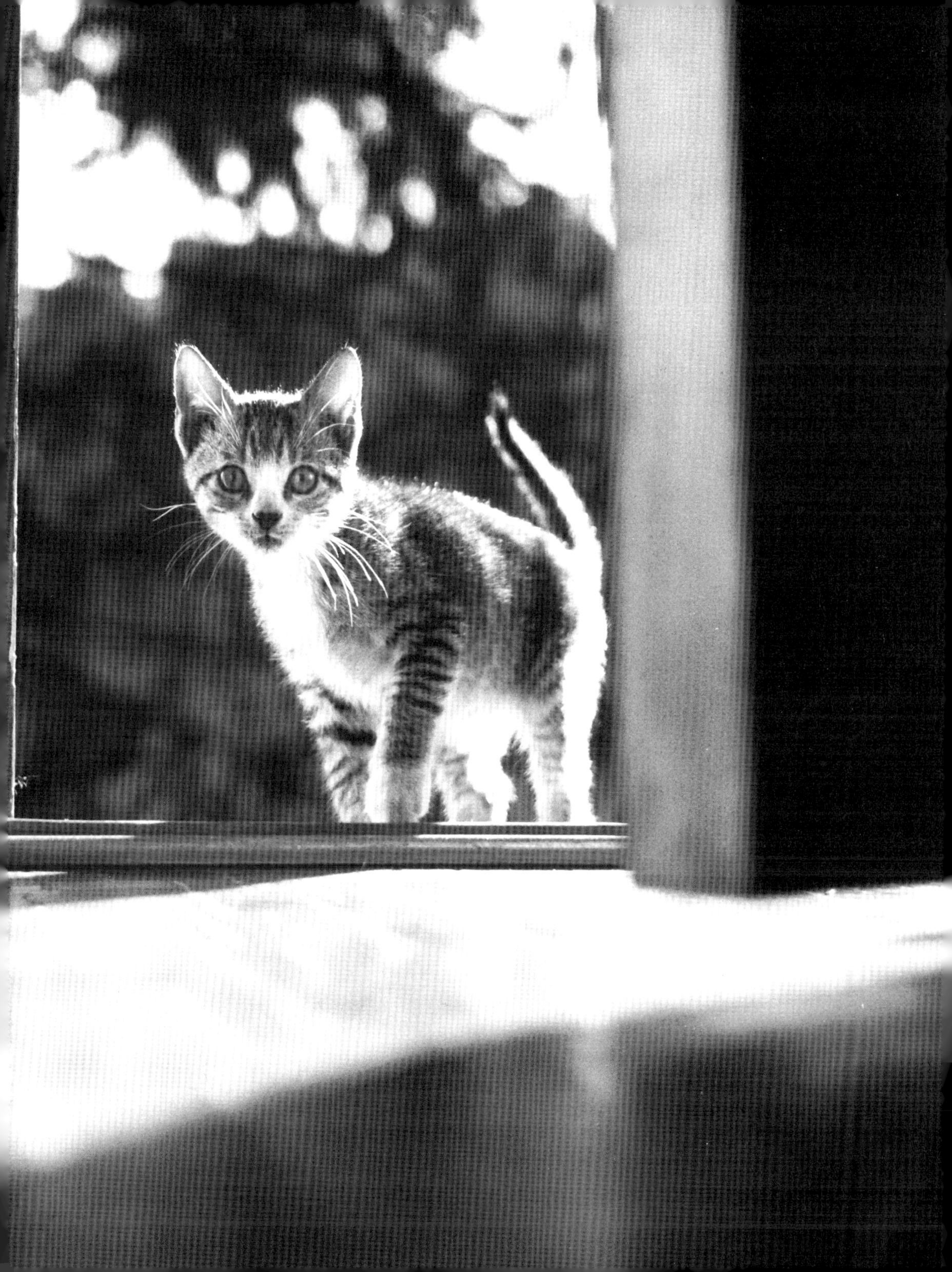

WALTER CHANDOHA

Family Cats

FROM THE ARCHIVE 1949–1962

Photographs © 2026 Walter Chandoha Archive
Foreword and Illustration © 2026 Grace Coddington

Special thanks to Leslie Simitch

Published by Damiani Books
info@damianibooks.com
www.damianibooks.com

Printed in February 2026, Italy.

ISBN 978-88-6208-858-9